Wheel of Mystery Quilts

Surprising Designs from a Classic Block

Helen Marshall

Martingale®
& COMPANY

Wheel of Mystery Quilts:
Surprising Designs from a Classic Block
© 2006 by Helen Marshall

That Patchwork Place® is an imprint
of Martingale & Company®.

Martingale & Company
20205 144th Avenue NE
Woodinville, WA 98072-8478 USA
www.martingale-pub.com

Printed in China
11 10 09 08 07 06   8 7 6 5 4 3 2 1

Library of Congress Cataloging-in-Publication Data
Marshall, Helen.
   Wheel of mystery quilts : surprising designs from
a classic block / Helen Marshall.
      p. cm.
   ISBN 1-56477-633-6
 1. Patchwork—Patterns. 2. Quilting—Patterns.
I. Title.
   TT835.M2735 2006
   746.46'041—dc22

                                        2005028409

Mission Statement

**Dedicated to providing quality products
and service to inspire creativity.**

Credits

President: Nancy J. Martin
CEO: Daniel J. Martin
VP and General Manager: Tom Wierzbicki
Publisher: Jane Hamada
Editorial Director: Mary V. Green
Managing Editor: Tina Cook
Technical Editor: Laurie Baker
Copy Editor: Sheila Chapman Ryan
Design Director: Stan Green
Illustrator: Laurel Strand
Cover and Text Designer: Regina Girard
Photographer: Brent Kane

Dedication

To my husband, Rodney, and our family

Acknowledgments

Even though my name is on the cover, there are a lot of people who have made this book possible. All of them deserve recognition for the encouragement they gave me that brought this book to fruition:

My husband, Rodney, who over the years has said constantly, "That will be good for the book";

My students, from whom I get a lot of new ideas;

The teachers with whom I've been fortunate to study;

My first embroidery teacher, Betty Logan, who opened my eyes to color, design, and techniques;

Joan Bright, who introduced me to patchwork;

Jan Beaney and Jean Littlejohn, who made it possible for me to study for my Part II City and Guilds vocational qualification in Windsor, England, and have encouraged this "alien" along the way;

Peter and David Mancuso, who asked me to teach at their quilt festivals and then to be the coordinator who sends quilts from New Zealand to their World Quilt & Textile shows in the United States;

Sharon Pederson, for encouraging me to write the book;

My friends, who have been supportive during this whole journey and were understanding when I was "otherwise engaged" in this project;

And finally, Martingale & Company staff, for believing in me. Without you this would not have happened.

Special thanks go to the following for their contributions to the book:

Dorothy Brown, Ami Simms, and Pepper Cory, for fabric;

Lyndsey Blaymires, Lorraine Bradley, Marge Hurst, Chris Kenna, and Timothe Mansfield, who made quilts for the gallery;

Bary Scott, for machine quilting five of the quilts.

~ Helen ~

Contents

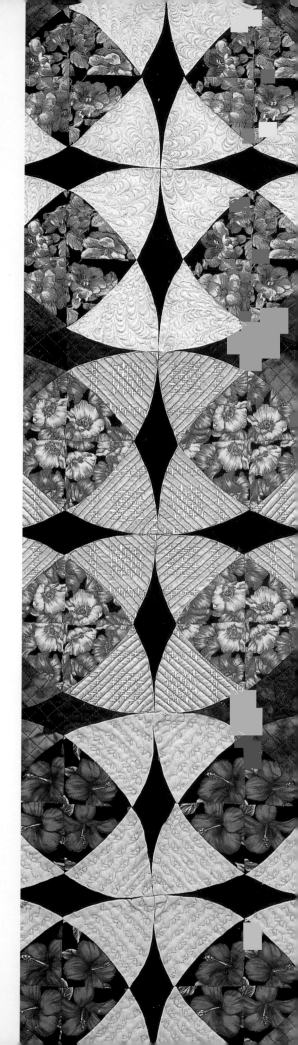

Preface

 This book would never have happened if I weren't surrounded by people who believed in me. My mother and grandmother, who were always nifty with a needle, encouraged me to sew. My husband, Rodney, and daughter and son, Catherine and Neil, always believed that I could sew costumes for school plays or drapes for the school hall, make knapsacks, mend tents, teach in faraway countries, and master the finer skills of embroidery. "Go for it, you can do it!" has always been a family cry.

I don't recall a quilt in my childhood, but there were always plenty of beautiful embroidered and knitted items for me to wear. From a relatively early age I was encouraged to sew clothes for my dolls and then for myself for special occasions. I married early and with a new home that needed furnishings, and later two children to clothe, my sewing machine was seldom idle.

As a stay-at-home mom, I attended embroidery classes, which led to patchwork classes. One day at the beginning of the school year, my former embroidery teacher called to say her adult embroidery class was overbooked and would I like to teach a new class with the extra students? I shudder to think of my lack of preparation (two days) and the hurried content of that class; however, that experience set me on the road to teaching embroidery and patchwork.

I've learned so much from all the hundreds of students that I've had in my classes over the past three decades, and there always seem to be new avenues to explore. Being in the right place at the right time has opened many doors for me, and I've been fortunate to take my teaching to many interesting places and meet wonderful people along the way.

So, now it's on to another phase—writing this book and sharing some tricks and tips I've picked up over the years. I hope you enjoy the journey and will share photographs of your quilts with me.

~ Helen ~

Introduction

Have you been fascinated with the Wheel of Mystery block but scared off because of its curved seams? If you're an accurate cutter and piecer, constructing this block will not be a problem. I'll share all the tips and tricks with you that I've learned through making dozens of these blocks. The mystery has been solved!

You won't need any special tools to make the quilts in this book, but I do encourage you to read through the "General Instructions" (page 8) so you can make sure you have everything you need. You'll also want to review that section for information on making the templates and cutting out the pieces, which is necessary for every project in the book.

The instructions for making the Wheel of Mystery block start on page 18. Here's where you will learn the step-by-step procedure for putting the pieces together so that you'll have nice, flat, accurately sewn blocks to assemble into a quilt top.

With that knowledge in hand, you'll be ready to delve into the projects. When I was designing the quilts for this book, there was no shortage of ideas. The versatility of this block lends itself to many different designs and effects. Just by changing the placement of block and background fabrics, new looks can be achieved, scalloped edges can be formed, and secondary patterns will be revealed. Be sure to look through the photographs in the "Gallery" (page 31) for even more ways the blocks can be assembled to create fabulous-looking quilts. This block has been around for a long time, but I hope you will experiment with it and find new and vibrant ways to use it.

General Instructions

 This section covers the basics of making a quilt top—fabrics, tools, templates, and cutting methods. You'll learn how to piece the Wheel of Mystery block in "Wheel of Mystery Block Construction" (page 18), and how to finish your quilt in "Finishing Techniques" (page 22).

FABRIC SELECTION AND CARE

A quilt often begins with the fabric you spied at your local quilt shop and just had to have. It's funny how fabric calls out to you, isn't it? Before you know it, several fabrics have talked to you, and you suddenly have what quilters commonly refer to as a "stash." This section will give you some helpful advice for selecting and preparing the fabrics for your quilt, whether they come from your collection or are newly purchased.

When you are selecting fabrics, protect your time and investment by choosing good quality, 100%-cotton fabrics from a reputable manufacturer. These fabrics typically have a tighter weave and are generally more colorfast than lesser-quality fabrics. I would especially like to stress the importance of a tight weave when making the quilts in this book. The width of the piece at the center of the Wheel of Mystery block is only ½". Believe me, if your fabric is loosely woven, it is more inclined to fray, and you will not relish the sewing experience. You invest a lot of your time into a quilt, and the initial outlay on good quality fabrics will produce a quilt that is easy to sew and that will provide pleasure for a long time.

If you have difficulty choosing fabrics, start with the main fabric—the one you couldn't leave in the shop. Now, look for some fat quarters that match. (You can invest in yardage after you've determined which fabrics to use.) As you are looking for fabrics, you need to remember two rules. First, include fabrics in light, medium, and dark values for good contrast. Second, be sure you have an assortment of small-, medium-, and large-scale prints for interest. Solid-colored fabrics and tone-on-tone prints should also be considered in your mix. They can provide just the right amount of contrast for busy prints, giving the eye a place to rest. Tone-on-tone prints, such as batiks and hand-dyed fabrics, are also good companions for more distinct prints. They provide more texture than a solid while still providing a calming effect.

Light-value, medium-value, and dark-value fabrics

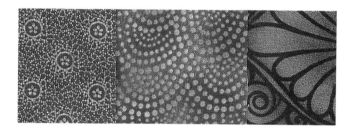

Small-scale, medium-scale, and large-scale prints

Tone-on-tone batiks and hand-dyed fabrics

From the group of fabrics you have selected, determine which fabrics you'd like to try using for the main pieces. Cut out several of these pieces and put them up on your design wall. You can now audition fabrics for the background.

Kick It Up!

Many years ago, Constance Howard, a wonderful embroidery teacher, told me that turquoise, burgundy, and swamp green would add pizzazz to any work of art. I have since added yellow to that list. Small quantities of any one of these colors are all that is needed to add color and sparkle to a quilt. Try it!

As you are deciding which fabrics to use and where to use them, remember that the *proportion* of prints and values is also important. You will be more pleased with the results if you use unequal proportions of the different color values and scales rather than equal amounts.

If you're still having difficulty, consult a good book on color, such as *Color: The Quilter's Guide* by Christine Barnes (That Patchwork Place, 1997). (This book is out of print, but a library or used-book shop might have it.) Understanding the relationships between colors is sometimes all you need to make your quilts outstanding.

A Spot of Color

Have you ever noticed those dots on the selvage of your fabrics? These are called color-registration dots. They show all the colors that were used to print the fabric, and are a good starting place for choosing coordinating colors for your quilt. Try not to match the colors exactly. A shade or two lighter or darker will provide better contrast.

I always prewash my fabrics, especially dark fabrics in which the dye might run. After washing, I test each fabric by wetting a small piece and ironing it on a paper towel. If there is any sign of dye on the paper towel, I rewash or put the fabric aside to use for a wall quilt that won't be washed or for some other project. Retayne, an anti-bleeding rinse that "fixes" or sets dyes on cotton to prevent color bleeding during washing, is a good product to use if any of your fabrics bleed. I had a fabric run in one of my quilts when I used a square of fabric that had not been prewashed; it bled onto some machine embroidery. Fortunately, it was near the edge, so the quilt ended up oblong instead of square! You may wonder why I'm emphasizing prewashing: accidents happen, so don't tell yourself that your quilt will never get wet.

Prewashing also prevents unexpected shrinking later on and gets rid of any chemicals the manufacturer may have used on the fabric. Some of the chemicals make the fabric stiff, which is not bad because it makes the fabric easier to cut and sew. To regain some of that stiffness, I often use spray starch when pressing the washed and dried fabrics.

TOOLS AND TOYS

When I started making quilts in the '70s, all of the pieces were cut out with scissors! It's hard to believe the difference the rotary cutter, self-healing mat, and specialty rulers have made to our craft. Of course, other time-saving and nifty tools have also been introduced, and although they are nice to have, you won't need all of them. Do try and keep the following basic items on hand to make your quilting life easier. As with most things in life, the better the tool, the more expensive it will be. Evaluate your budget and purchase the best quality tools you can afford.

⁜ **Rotary-cutting equipment.** You will need a rotary cutter with a retractable blade that is at least 45 mm in diameter for cutting strips and other straight pieces. For cutting around curves, use a rotary cutter with a 28-mm retractable blade. The blades are very sharp, so be sure you practice good safety habits when using them, and always keep the cutters away from children.

To protect your table and keep your rotary-cutter blade sharp, always rotary cut on a self-healing mat. There are several sizes available, but I find that an 18" x 24" mat is just the right size to cut a width of fabric folded into four layers, yet not too big to take to a class. Mats should be stored flat and out of direct sunlight to prevent warping.

Clear acrylic rulers are necessary for accurate cutting. There are many sizes and brands of rulers available. Choose rulers with lines that are easy to read. For the projects in this book, I would suggest that you have three sizes on hand: 6" x 12", 6" x 24", and 8" square.

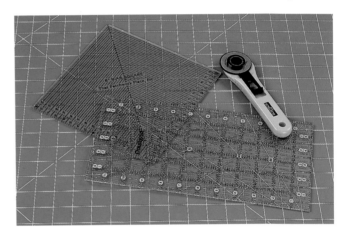

Rotary-cutting mat, rulers, and cutter

⁜ **Sewing machine.** You don't need a machine with all the bells and whistles for these quilts; a reliable machine in good working order that makes an even, straight stitch and a closely spaced zigzag stitch (satin stitch) is sufficient. If you want to free-motion machine quilt, you will also need to be able to drop or cover the feed dogs. A large, flat sewing surface will make your sewing easier and more comfortable. You can achieve this by setting your machine into a sewing machine table or attaching an extension table to the machine's free arm. Make sure you clean your machine after every project and oil it with good-quality machine oil when needed.

Sewing-machine presser feet. There are several specialty presser feet that will make sewing the projects in this book easier. A ¼" foot is helpful for achieving an accurate seam allowance when piecing. For satin stitching some of the embroidered embellishments, use an open-toe appliqué foot or embroidery foot. If you decide to machine quilt your project, you will need a darning foot, an open-toe darning foot, a free-motion quilting foot, or a walking or even-feed foot. A zipper foot is needed to make the piping that is applied to some of the quilt edges. Check with your sewing-machine dealer for the correct foot for your needs.

Sewing-machine needles. Machine needles come in a vast array of types and sizes. I suggest you use a size 70/11 or 80/12 Sharp for piecing. Other needles are available for working with specialty threads or doing specific tasks, such as embroidery or quilting. In general, avoid using universal needles; they are halfway between a ballpoint and a Sharp and are not suitable for piecing or quilting. I usually change the needle at the beginning of each new project unless it has been recently replaced.

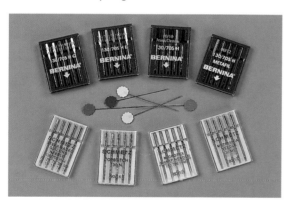

Pins. Flower-head pins are good to use when you are fussy cutting block pieces because they lie flat and you can easily place your template over them. Lace pins have a thinner shaft than other pins and can help you match points accurately. If you have difficulty finding lace pins, silk pins will also work. T-shaped pins are needed when blocking the quilt.

Thread. Like fabric, this is another area in which you don't want to skimp on quality. Good-quality cotton or polyester 50-weight, 3-ply thread is ideal for piecing. Because I'm an embroiderer as well as a quilter, I always try to match the thread color of one of the fabrics in the project for the piecing process. For quilting, your thread can be cotton, silk, rayon, or metallic, and vary in size from 30 to 100 weight. The thicker the thread, the lower the size number will be, and the more pronounced the quilting stitch will be.

Design wall. Over the years I've successfully laid out a great many quilts on the floor, but a design wall makes the process much easier. My design wall is actually two 6' x 3' boards that I've covered with flannel, but something as simple as a piece of flannel draped over a door works as well.

Iron and ironing board. A small iron and board is great to keep next to your machine for pressing seams. However, you will need a full-sized iron and ironing board or other large pressing surface for pressing blocks and your quilt top.

Spray starch. I use spray starch for adding body to the fabrics after laundering, and for pressing blocks.

Template-making materials. There are two types of templates used in this book: block templates and window templates. You'll need tracing paper and heavyweight cardboard to make the block templates. The window templates for fussy cutting can be made from lightweight cardboard. Use paper scissors for cutting the tracing paper and a craft knife for cutting through cardboard. Double-sided adhesive tape is also helpful for adhering the traced patterns to the cardboard before cutting out the templates.

Seam ripper and tweezers. There is always a need for a bit of "reverse sewing," so keep a seam ripper close to your machine. Pick up pesky wisps of cut threads with the tweezers.

- ✤ **Small scissors or snips.** A small, sharp pair of scissors or thread snips can come in handy for trimming threads. My favorite snips have a curved blade and come from Havel's. For more information, see "Resources" (page 95).

- ✤ **Retractable metal tape measure.** Because it doesn't stretch like a cloth tape measure, I find that this is the most efficient and accurate way of measuring a quilt for borders.

- ✤ **Reducing glass.** After you've laid out your block pieces on your design wall, this little tool can help you see the whole quilt as you would from a distance and give you a better idea of the overall look of the design. A security peephole, available at home-improvement stores, also works for this purpose, as does looking through a camera lens or the "wrong" end of a pair of binoculars.

- ✤ **Marking pens and pencils.** You will need a soft lead pencil or chalk pencil to mark fussy-cut pieces of the block, and a fine-point black pen or marker to trace the patterns onto tracing paper and to trace the templates onto cardboard.

- ✤ **Fabric pens.** If you have a motif on the fabric that is too pale, fabric pens can work magic to boost the color. A few of the flowers in "Aloha" (page 65) were doctored this way!

- ✤ **Self-adhesive labels.** When your blocks are in the desired position on your design wall, number them with removable self-adhesive labels (¾"-diameter dots work well) or a sticky note to remind you of the order after you've taken them down.

- ✤ **Mirror tiles.** I like to use two 10" mirror tiles to help me see how a fussy-cut portion of the fabric will look when it is repeated in the finished block. Lay the two mirrors right sides together and tape one edge together in several spots to form hinges.

CUTTING YOUR FABRIC

All of the pieces for your quilt will be cut with a rotary cutter. The block pieces require templates that you will cut around, but unless you are fussy cutting the pieces, you can cut strips for these pieces first. Fussy-cut pieces will be cut after all of the strips are cut.

Border strips and some binding strips will be cut on the lengthwise grain (if they're not bias strips) for stability. I like to cut them from my fabric before I cut the template pieces. The project instructions will indicate the width the strips should be cut. If I am working with striped or checked fabrics, I cut these strips out with scissors. That way I can follow the pattern when cutting and sewing. Other strips can be cut across the width of the fabric.

Crosswise Strips

1. Fold the fabric in half along the lengthwise grain, matching the selvage edges; smooth out the wrinkles. Fold the fabric in half again along the lengthwise grain; smooth out the wrinkles. With the double fold closest to you, lay a rectangular ruler on the right-hand end of the fabric. Align a horizontal line of the ruler with the double-fold edge. Position the ruler only as far in from the raw edges as needed to cut through all of the layers of fabric. Cut along the long edge of the ruler. Always cut away from yourself. Discard the cut piece.

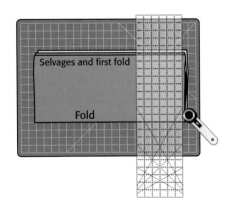

Selvages and first fold

Fold

2. Rotate the fabric or mat so the straightened edge is to your left. You are now ready to cut strips. Align the correct measurement line of your ruler with the previously cut edge of the fabric. Cut the strip along the right side of the ruler. Continue cutting as many fabric strips as required for the project.

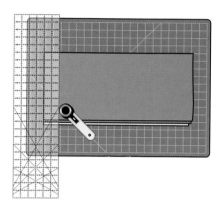

Tip

If you have a free-standing cutting surface, position your cutting board on one corner. Then, if needed, you can easily walk around the corner and complete your cuts without moving the fabric.

Lengthwise Strips

1. Fold the fabric in half along the crosswise grain, matching the selvage edges; smooth out the wrinkles. Fold the fabric in half again along the crosswise grain; smooth out the wrinkles. With the double fold closest to you, lay a rectangular ruler on the right-hand end of the fabric. Align a horizontal line of the ruler with the double-fold edge. Position the ruler only as far in from the raw edges as needed to cut through all of the layers of fabric and remove the selvages.

Cut along the long edge of the ruler. Always cut away from yourself. Discard the cut piece.

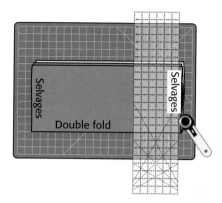

2. Rotate the fabric or mat so the straightened edge is to your left. You are now ready to cut strips. Align the correct measurement line of your ruler with the previously cut edge of the fabric. Cut the strip along the right side of the ruler. Continue cutting as many fabric strips as required for the project.

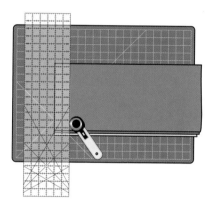

Template Pieces

You will be using templates to cut the pieces for the Wheel of Mystery blocks. If the template pieces are cut from the same fabric as the border and/or binding strips, the template pieces are cut last. Template pieces can be fussy cut or not, depending on the look you desire.

For fussy-cut pieces, you will choose the part of the fabric pattern you want to feature and then cut four matching pieces from the fabric, disregarding the grain-line arrow marked on the template. Depending on the look I want, I will fussy cut either the A or B template pieces. This may seem like an extravagant way to use fabric, but usually there is little fabric left over. When you are selecting fabrics and you know you want to fussy cut the pieces, check the number of repeats across the width and length of the fabric and take this into account when purchasing yardage. You can see examples of fussy-cut pieces in "Pansy Posies" (page 42), in which several different motifs were fussy cut from one fabric, and in "Aloha" (page 65), in which several different fabrics were fussy cut for the "wheels."

For non-fussy-cut pieces, I find that it is easier to cut a strip ¼" to ½" wider than the template and then cut out the pieces through all four layers. Because of the template curves, cutting through more than four layers just isn't accurate enough. The project instructions will not specify to cut strips but you are welcome to do so. Follow the grain-line arrow when positioning the template on the fabric.

PRESSING

I always press my seams open because I find that it produces flatter blocks and ultimately a flatter quilt. I'm aware that most American quilters press the seams to one side, usually toward the darker fabric. Press whichever way you are more comfortable with, but please try my method first. I like to set my seams first by pressing the seam to one side on the right side of the joined pieces using a dry iron. Then I press the seam open on the wrong side. To prevent the block edges from being distorted, I don't use steam until the quilt top is completed. Remember to move the iron up and down, not back and forth, to prevent stretching the pieces out of shape.

When you are sewing pressed-open seams, pin down the seam that is facing the needle so it is less likely to get turned back as the needle goes across it.

MAKING THE TEMPLATES

There are two types of templates used in this book: the templates for the blocks, and the window templates for fussy cutting. You will find the template patterns starting on page 87. The ¼" seam allowance has already been added, and the points have been clipped to make joining the seams easier. At the beginning of the cutting instructions for each project, you will find a list of the exact templates required.

Block Templates

1. Trace the desired patterns onto tracing paper using a fine-line marker. Leave at least ½" between each shape. Mark the grain-line arrow and template letter on each shape. Roughly cut out the templates at least ¼" outside the marked lines. (The excess will be trimmed away later.) Apply double-sided adhesive tape to the

wrong side of each shape within the marked lines.

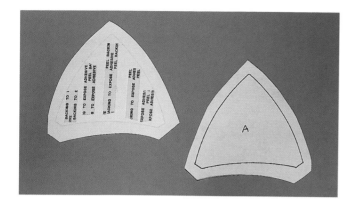

2. Adhere each shape to a piece of heavy cardboard. I prefer to use heavy cardboard to make the templates, rather than template plastic, because cardboard is less likely to be sliced by the rotary cutter as you are cutting out the fabric pieces. Use a craft knife to cut out the templates on the traced lines.

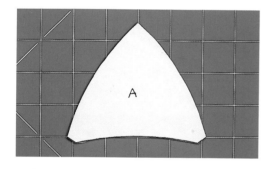

3. Place each template over the original pattern to make sure it is an exact match.

Window Templates

A window template is essential when you want to fussy cut one of the block pieces. It will ensure that all of your pieces are cut from the same portion of the fabric pattern.

To make the window template, make the desired block template as described above. Center the template on a piece of lightweight cardboard and trace around it (template A is shown in the photograph). Use your craft knife to cut out the shape; discard the cut-out shape. The opening in the cardboard will be used to isolate parts of the fabric that you think will be suitable for fussy cutting. Specific instructions for fussy cutting are given below.

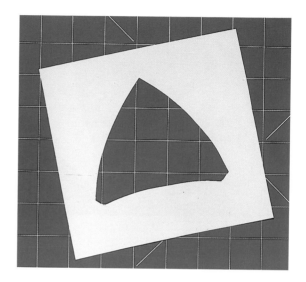

FUSSY CUTTING

Fussy cutting is when you isolate a particular motif in your fabric and cut it out. Look through the pictures of the quilts in this book and you can see how some of the projects used fussy cutting to create interesting effects. Using one of the window templates, you will need to cut out four identical motifs. Don't worry about grain line for fussy-cut pieces. Pieces that connect to the fussy-cut pieces will be cut on-grain and will provide enough stability to keep the blocks from stretching.

Note: The yardage given in the project instructions for fussy-cut pieces is approximate, based on the fabric I used. To determine the actual yardage required for the fabric you intend to use, measure the distance from one motif to the same motif along the selvage. This is called the pattern repeat. The pattern will also repeat across the width of the fabric. Check to see how many pieces you get across the width of the fabric within one selvage-to-selvage repeat and then determine how many repeats you will need to cut the required number of pieces.

1. Move the window template for the desired piece across the fabric until you see a portion that looks suitable.

2. Use a chalk pencil to trace around the inner edges of the template. Remove the template.

3. Cut out the piece approximately ¼" to ½" beyond the marked line. This excess allows you some additional room for aligning pieces later and will eventually be trimmed away.

4. Find another identical motif on your fabric. Place the cut-out piece over the motif, matching the pattern as well as you can. Use your chalk pencil to mark around the cut-out piece. Remove the cut-out piece and cut out the shape you just traced around. Repeat twice to cut out a total of four identical pieces.

Tip

Two mirror tiles taped together along one edge make a useful tool for showing how the four repeated pieces will look when they are sewn together.

5. With right sides up, stack all four pieces together, aligning the edges. Insert a pin into an easily identifiable part of the motif through all of the layers. Do this in three different places.

6. Lift up the top piece and check to be sure the pins are going through the exact same spot on the second layer as the first. Make any needed adjustments. Repeat with the third and fourth layers, being careful that the pins remain in all four layers.

7. When all of the pieces line up exactly, pin the layers together, inserting the new pins at a right angle to each alignment pin. Use pins with flat heads for this step so the trimming that you do later will be more accurate. Remove the alignment pins.

8. Position the corresponding template over the pinned pieces. Again, disregard the template grain line. Use your rotary cutter to trim the pieces to the exact size of the template. Be careful not to run your blade over any of the pins.

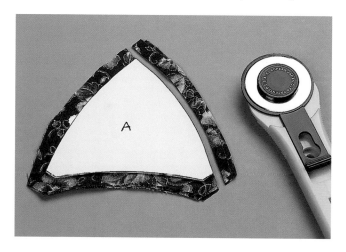

Wheel of Mystery Block Construction

 The Wheel of Mystery block is the basis for all of the projects in this book. Some variations of this block are used as well; instructions for those blocks are given with the project.

When constructing the Wheel of Mystery block, the most important things to remember are that your seam allowance must be exactly ¼" and that you must thoroughly press the seam after each piece is added. Before beginning your project, make a sample block and be sure the finished block measures 7½" square. For smoother curves, set your machine for a shorter-than-normal stitch length.

Many of the projects instruct you to pin the pieces for the quilt top to your design wall before you assemble the blocks so you can make sure you are pleased with the overall design. I find that it is easier to transport the pieces for one block at a time to my sewing machine by placing them on a piece of template plastic that has been lightly sprayed with temporary basting spray. The basting spray keeps the pieces in order without leaving a sticky residue.

Note: I used a contrasting thread for the samples in the following photographs so that the stitches could be clearly seen. You will want to use a thread that matches one of your fabrics.

1. With right sides together, pin a C piece to an A piece along one curved edge, matching and pinning at the ends. With the C piece on top, stitch the pieces together.

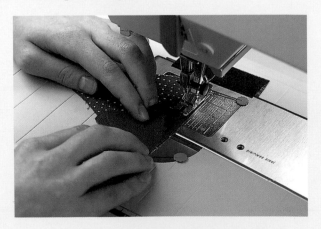

2. Snip the seam 1" from the outside edge (the widest part of the C piece). You will now have a long and a short portion of seam.

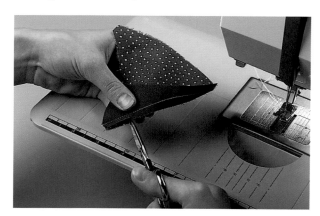

3. Using a dry iron, press the short portion of the seam open and the long portion toward the A piece as shown. This pressing strategy will remove the bulk when joining the pieces.

Tip

I prefer not to use steam at all when I'm pressing the pieces because it tends to stretch bias edges. I do use steam to press the completed block.

4. Join an A piece to the other side of the C piece as shown to complete an ACA unit. Clip and press the seam as before.

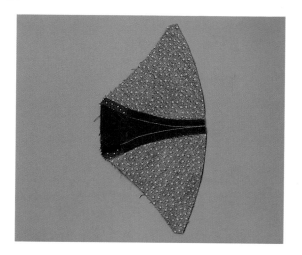

5. From the right side, thoroughly press the intersection where the three pieces meet and the C piece comes to a point.

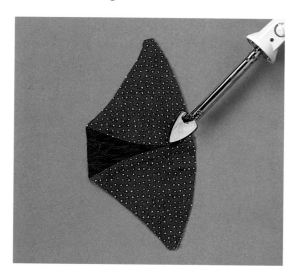

6. Repeat steps 1–5 to make an additional ACA unit.

7. Join the remaining two C pieces at the narrow ends as shown, leaving a thread tail at the beginning and end of the seam. Because this is such a short seam, it can come apart easily if the threads are clipped now. Press the seam open.

Tip

Start and stop sewing on a small piece of folded fabric to keep your machine from gobbling the beginning and end of your seams.

8. Sew the joined C pieces to one ACA unit, matching the center seams and ends. Press the seam toward the ACA unit, first from the wrong side and then from the right side, checking to be sure there are no folds on the right side. This seam needs to be well pressed because the next seam will run very, very close to it, and it's possible to catch a little bit of the previously sewn ACA unit. Then it's stitch-ripping time!

9. Repeat step 10 to sew the remaining ACA unit to the other side of the joined C pieces. As you approach the center, stitch close to, but not over, the previous row of stitching. Press, then clip the thread tails that you left when you joined the C units. You should not see any part of the C pieces at the center of the block when you press the seam.

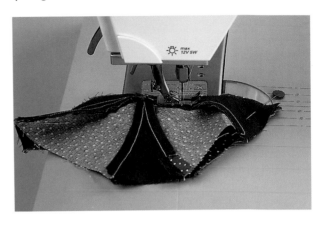

Tip

I've found that it's a good idea to sew the portion of the seam where all the pieces meet with a basting stitch first to check that the sewing line is in the correct place. If it is, then I go back and stitch with a regular-length stitch.

10. Refer to step 2 to clip the seams joining the A and C pieces that have not already been clipped.

11. Pin the B pieces to the remaining side of each A piece. With the A piece on top, stitch the pieces together. Press the seams open.

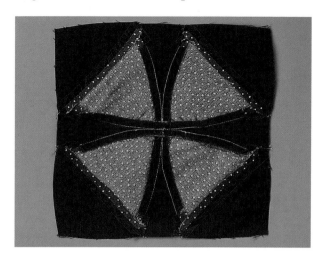

sides of the block as you press to make it fit the marked square. All the hills and valleys should become flat and you should have a perfectly square block that requires little, if any, trimming.

Trim your block if it is too large.

12. Press the block. It should measure 7½" square, but don't panic if it's a little larger or smaller. If your blocks are larger than 7½", use an 8" square ruler to trim the blocks, being careful not to cut off any points and making sure there is ¼" seam allowance beyond the points. If your blocks are too small, draw a 7½" square onto a piece of preshrunk nonfusible interfacing and then pin the marked interfacing to your ironing board. Apply spray starch to the block, and then pin it to the interfacing, aligning two adjacent sides of the block with the marked lines. Using steam, press the block, pulling on the unpinned

If it is too small, press your block to fit a 7½" square.

Finishing Techniques

After the quilt top is finished, it's ready to be layered with batting and backing, and then to be quilted and bound. This section will explain these processes, as well as provide information about adding a hanging sleeve and a quilt label.

BACKING

The quilting process will go much smoother if you choose a good quality quilting fabric for the backing. Try to avoid fabrics with a high thread count, especially if you are hand quilting, because they are hard to quilt through.

Your backing should be cut 6" longer and wider than your quilt top. If your quilt top is wider than 36", you'll need to join two fabric pieces to make a large-enough backing. Prewash and dry the fabric first and then remove the selvages. Cut the fabric in half across the width and sew the two pieces together. If there is a definite pattern, match it when joining the pieces. If you want to avoid seaming your backing, extra-wide fabrics are available and marketed specifically for backings.

Tip

The lengthwise fabric grain has the least amount of stretch, so I like to use it for the length of the quilt. Match the grain lines of your backing and quilt top for the most stable quilt.

BATTING

There are many types of batting. The one you choose depends on your quilting method and the end use of the quilt. I used cotton batting for the quilts in this book because they were all machine quilted, and I find that there is less slipping with cotton batting. I use low-loft cotton batting for most of my quilts, unless I am making a quilt for a child. In that case, I use polyester batting, which is less likely to suffer through a lot of laundering.

Unpack your batting the day before you layer the quilt to allow the folds to relax. Cut the batting the same size as the quilt backing (6" longer and 6" wider than the quilt top).

MARKING

Before you can begin the layering process, decide on the quilt design. If you plan to have a complex design, you will need to mark the quilt top before it is layered. There are several tools you can use for marking—chalk pencils, water-soluble markers, or lead pencils, to name a few. Test the tool you intend to use on scraps of your fabric before you mark the quilt top to be sure the marks can be easily removed when you are finished. You do not need to mark the top if you are free-motion quilting or straight-line quilting.

LAYERING

It is now time to layer the backing, batting, and quilt top in preparation for quilting.

1. Thoroughly press the quilt top and backing to eliminate any wrinkles. If you have not already done so, press open the joining seam (if any) on the backing.

2. Lay the backing, wrong side up, on a large, flat surface and smooth out any wrinkles. Without stretching the backing, use masking tape to fasten the backing to the surface.

3. Lay the batting over the backing. Smooth out any wrinkles.

4. Center the pressed quilt top, right side up, on the batting and smooth out any wrinkles. Be sure that all of the layers are oriented in the correct direction.

Tip

I have two trestle tables that I butt up next to each other to make a large-enough surface for layering my quilts. To help me keep the layers aligned, I tape a toothpick to the center of each table side so that it extends past the edge. When I am centering the layers, I just feel for the toothpicks.

5. If you're going to machine quilt, I suggest you use rustproof 1" safety pins to hold the layers together. Start pinning at the center and work out to all four edges, placing pins 3" apart. This will divide the quilt into quarters. Now, pin each quarter, working from the center out.

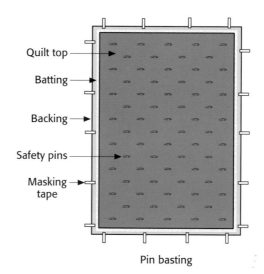

Quilt top

Batting

Backing

Safety pins

Masking tape

Pin basting

For hand quilting, thread basting is a better option than pin basting. Always use white thread so there isn't any chance of thread dye transferring to your top. Using a long needle, start at the center and work 1"-long stitches out

to all four edges. Repeat across the surface of the quilt at 3" to 4" intervals.

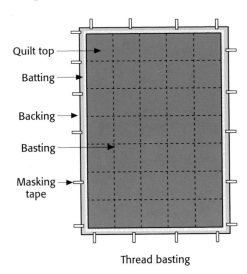

Thread basting

6. Fold the excess batting and backing to the front to get it out of the way. Pin or stitch close to the quilt-top edges to secure the excess and stabilize the edge.

QUILTING

Quilting is a vast subject that can't be covered in its entirety in a few paragraphs. If this is a subject you need help with, I recommend that you look for guidance in any of the wonderful books that deal specifically with quilting. In the meantime, I will briefly share the three machine quilting methods that I use the most—straight-line quilting, free-motion quilting, and decorative-stitch quilting. Of course, you can also choose to quilt by hand.

I like to begin by stabilizing the quilt with straight stitching alongside the seam of several horizontal and vertical rows. If I don't want these lines to be part of the quilting, I use water-soluble thread, which will dissolve when I wash the quilt.

Straight-line quilting includes any quilting design that utilizes straight lines. Crosshatching and grids are included in this method. Stitching in the ditch is not recommended because the seams

are pressed open. Use a walking foot, even-feed foot, or the even-feed feature on your machine to evenly feed both layers through the machine and prevent folds in your quilting.

Walking foot

Many times I replace straight lines with one of the built-in decorative stitches on my sewing machine. Use your walking foot or even-feed foot for this treatment as well.

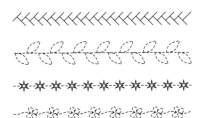

Free-motion quilting allows you, not the machine, to control the stitching. You can create virtually any design that you want. Drop the feed dogs so you can move the quilt in any direction. Use a darning foot or open-toe darning foot to allow movement of the layers.

Darning foot   Open-toe darning foot

BLOCKING

After the quilt has been quilted, it needs to be blocked to ensure that it is square.

1. Trim off the excess batting and backing to within ½" of the quilt edges (this isn't the final trim).

2. Lay the quilt on a flat surface and spray it with water to dampen it. Let the water sink into the quilt.

3. Using T-shaped pins, pin the quilt directly into your design wall or into towel-covered carpet, stretching as needed to square up and flatten the quilt. Let the quilt dry.

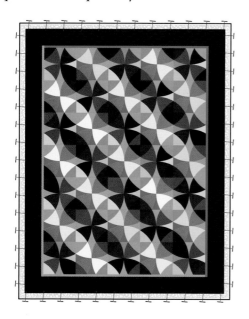

4. Remove the quilt from the design wall or carpet. Trim away the excess batting and backing, leaving enough to fill the binding. I usually trim ¼" from the final edge of the quilt top for a ½" finished binding.

PIPING

Adding piping to your quilt top before adding the binding can give your quilt a tailored look. You will need thin cord (string will also work) that's the length of your quilt edges plus an additional 10", and a 1½"-wide straight-cut or bias-cut fabric strip

the length of the cording or string (refer to "Curved Edges" on page 28 for information on cutting and joining bias strips). Preshrink the cord or string before cutting it to the required length.

1. To make the piping, place the cord on the wrong side of the fabric strip. Wrap one edge of the fabric strip over the cord and align the raw edge with the opposite side. Snug up the cord to the folded edge. Using your zipper foot, stitch close to, but not right up against, the cord. By leaving a little bit of space now, you will be able to prevent the stitching from showing after the binding is applied. Trim the seam allowance to ¼".

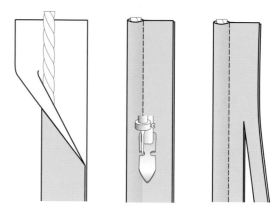

2. Measure through the vertical and horizontal centers of the quilt top. Cut two pieces of piping 2" longer than the horizontal measurement and two pieces 2" longer than the vertical measurement. Center the length of piping for the quilt top edge at the top of the quilt, aligning the long raw edges. Using your zipper foot, stitch over the previous line of stitching. Repeat for the bottom edge and then the sides. Trim the piping ends even with the quilt edges.

3. Refer to "Binding" (below) to apply the binding, using a zipper foot and stitching as close as possible to the piping cord.

BINDING

Binding your quilt is necessary to enclose the three layers and provide your quilt with a nice, finished look. The shape of the quilt's outer edges will determine whether you use straight-cut or bias-cut strips.

Straight Edges

Quilts with straight edges can be bound with straight-cut binding strips. This method creates a double-layer (French) binding.

1. Measure through the vertical and horizontal center of the quilt top and make a note of the measurements. Find the center point on each side of the quilt and mark it with a safety pin. For large quilts, I also mark the quarter points.

2. Refer to the project cutting instructions to cut the required number of binding strips across the width or length of the fabric. The number of strips is based on the measurement of the perimeter of the quilt plus an additional 10" for seams and mitered corners. The width of the strips used for each project will vary depending on the finished size of the quilt. If you are using a checked, plaid, or striped fabric, use scissors and follow the fabric's pattern.

3. With right sides together, sew the strips together on the bias as shown to create one long strip. Trim the seam allowance to ¼". Press the seams open.

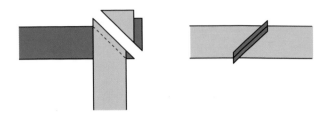

4. Press the binding strip in half lengthwise, wrong sides together. Starting in the middle of one side of the quilt, temporarily position the binding strip around the quilt to make sure that none of the seams will be at the corners of the quilt. It is difficult to make a nice miter with the additional bulk of a seam.

5. When you are pleased with the positioning of the strip, pin the binding to the quilt edge at the center mark on one side of the quilt, aligning the edges. Using the measurement you took in step 1, determine half the distance of the side you are working on. For larger quilts, you will also need to determine one quarter of the measurement. Measuring from the center pin, mark the distance(s) on the binding with another pin. Pin the binding in place, matching the binding pin that indicates half the distance with the quilt corner. If you marked the quarter point, match this pin with the safety pin you used in step 1 to mark the quarter point on the quilt top. Add additional pins as needed once these pins are in place. Begin stitching 8" from the end of the binding. Use a seam allowance that is ⅙ the cut width of the binding. For example, if you cut 3"-wide strips, your seam allowance will be ½". Stop stitching one seam-allowance width from the corner. Backstitch and remove the quilt from the machine.

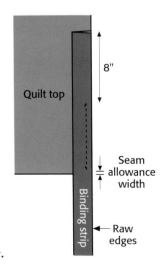

6. Turn the quilt so you're ready to sew the second side. Fold the binding up to create a 45°-angle fold. Hold the fold in place with your finger. Fold the loose binding strip down so the new fold is parallel to the first edge of the quilt and the raw edges are aligned with the second edge of the quilt. Referring to the measurement you took in step 1, determine the amount of binding needed for the side you are working on and mark the length with a pin. Place another pin at the center point of the binding. With the pins at the center and end of the binding aligned with the safety pins on the quilt, pin the binding in place. Remove the safety pins. Beginning at the folded edge, stitch as far as one seam allowance width from the next corner. Backstitch and remove the quilt from the machine.

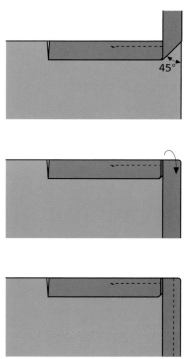

7. Repeat step 6 at each of the remaining corners. Stop stitching when you are 10" to 12" from the original starting point. Backstitch and remove the quilt from the machine. Cut the end of the binding strip so it overlaps the beginning of the binding strip by at least 5". Pin the ends together 3½" from the starting point. Clip the raw binding edges at the pin, being careful not

to cut past the seam allowance or into the quilt layers. Open up the binding and match the ends as shown. Stitch the ends together on the diagonal.

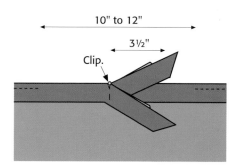

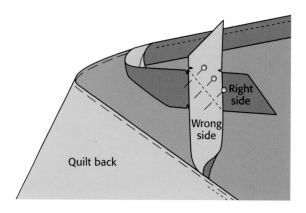

8. Fold the binding over the raw edge and slip-stitch the folded edge in place on the backing, mitering and stitching down the corners.

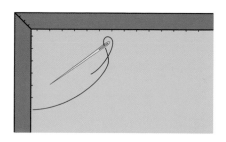

Curved Edges

If your quilt has curved edges, you will need to use bias-cut strips for a smooth binding.

1. To cut bias strips, align the 45°-angle marking of your rotary ruler with the selvage edge of a single layer of fabric that has been placed on your rotary-cutting mat. Cut along the right-hand edge of the ruler. From the cut edge, measure 2" and cut a strip. The project instructions will tell you how many inches of bias binding you will need. Cut the amount of strips needed to achieve this length when the strips are sewn together.

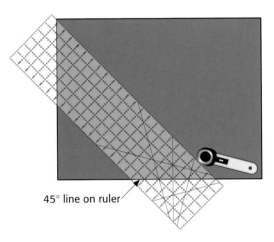

45° line on ruler

2. Join the strips as shown to make one long strip. Press the seams open.

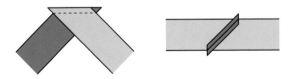

3. Press the binding strip in half lengthwise, wrong sides together.

4. *For quilts with rounded corners,* refer to step 1 of "Straight Edges" (page 26) to find the center of each side and mark it with a safety pin. Begin adding the binding as instructed in step 5 of "Straight Edges." Pin the binding around the first curve, taking care not to stretch the binding. Continue in this manner around the entire quilt and finish the binding as instructed in steps 7 and 8 of "Straight Edges."

5. *For quilts with scalloped edges,* stay stitch along the scallops a scant ¼" from the edge. Mark the inside corner point of the first scallop with a pin. Leaving a tail that will be long enough to join the ends in the center of the preceding scallop, begin stitching the binding to the quilt top edge at the center of the first scallop, aligning the raw edges. Stitch to the pin. With the needle down, raise the presser foot and pivot the quilt to start on the next scallop. When you are 10" to 12" from the beginning, measure and join the binding as instructed in step 7 of "Straight Edges."

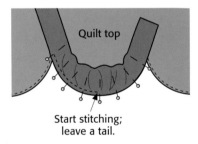

Quilt top

Start stitching; leave a tail.

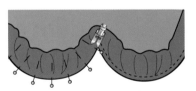

6. Turn the binding to the back of the quilt, one scallop at a time, mitering and stitching the inside corners.

Quilt back

ADDING A HANGING SLEEVE

If you plan on hanging your quilt on a wall, you will need to add a hanging sleeve to the backing. I prefer to add the sleeve after I've bound the quilt so that there isn't any additional bulk in the binding.

1. Cut a piece of backing fabric 1" less than the finished width of the quilt and 9" wide. This allows for a ¼" double hem on each end and positions the sleeve 1" in from the quilt sides.

2. Fold the fabric in half lengthwise, wrong sides together, matching the raw edges. Finger-press the fold.

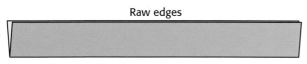

Raw edges

Finger-press.

3. Open the fabric so that the wrong side is facing up. Bring both raw edges in to meet the center fold; finger-press the outer edges. You will follow the new pressed lines to stitch the sleeve to the quilt back.

Finger-press.

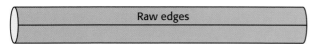

Raw edges

Finger-press.

4. Open up the fabric and fold it in half length-wise, right sides together, matching the raw edges. Stitch ¼" from the long, raw edge. Press the seam open. Turn the sleeve to the right side.

¼"

5. Turn under the short ends ¼" twice to create a double hem. Machine stitch the hems in place.

6. Position the long seam in the center of the tube. Center the sleeve on the back of the quilt so it butts up to the binding at the top of the quilt and the seam is facing the backing. The ends should be 1" from the sides.

1"   1"

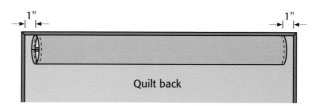

Quilt back

7. Pin; then stitch the sleeve in place along the top pressed line, stitching only through the backing and batting. Remove the pins. Push up the excess fabric and pin along the bottom pressed line. Stitch along the pressed line as before. The excess fabric will create a bulge that will accommodate the hanging rod. Stitch the bottom layer of the sleeve short ends in place.

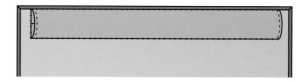

 Tip

I cut my hanging rod the same width as the sleeve, and then insert a screw eye into each end of the rod. I can then attach a string to the screw eyes and hang the quilt like a picture, or I can position nails on the wall for the screw eyes to slip over.

MAKING A LABEL

Be sure to add a label to your quilt back so future generations will know the quilt's story. At the very least, sign and date your quilt. Consider also including the city where the quilt was made, who it was given to or made for, and the occasion for making it, if applicable.

Here are several creative ways to make and embellish your labels.

⧉ If you have a sewing machine with programmable lettering, this is an easy way to create wording. I like to put the fabric into a hoop to keep it stable when I'm using this method. Use a thread color and font that matches the quilt.

⧉ Take a digital photograph of the quilt or the quilt's fabric, mask out the center of the photo, and add the words to the masked area.

⧉ Use a clip-art image that reflects the quilt, the recipient's interest, or the occasion for which the quilt was made, and then add the quilt information.

Passion Fruit

Helen Marshall

43" x 57"

**all cotton fabrics
and batting**

*Pansy Posies
Helen Marshall
33" x 33"
All cotton fabrics
and batting*

Blocks of Fun

**Helen Marshall
39" x 56¼"**

all cotton fabrics and batting

Gallery

Lordy, Miss Claudie, It's Gaudy! *by Helen Marshall, 36" x 36"*

This is the first quilt I made using the Wheel of Mystery templates. I made this quilt from African-print fabrics when I heard I had been invited to tutor at the Dais Symposium in Port Elizabeth, South Africa, in 1998. The background is a colorwashed batik fabric. I entered this in an "Ugly but Divine" competition—hence the title. "Japanese Fans" (page 60) is a smaller version of this quilt.

Tropical Flowers of the Night *by Helen Marshall, 34" x 34"*

This is the second quilt I made using the Wheel of Mystery templates. It has exactly the same number of blocks as "Lordy, Miss Claudie, It's Gaudy!" (page 31). This time, the petal-shaped pieces are fussy cut from the same piece of tropical floral fabric. The quilting pattern is a smaller version of the blocks and is done with a multicolored rayon thread.

Floating Circles *by Helen Marshall, 35" x 35"*

A carefully controlled color scheme gives this quilt the appearance of one layer of rings floating on top of a darker layer of rings. Feathers are the theme for the quilting. Timothe Mansfield created "Rims of Fire" (page 36) from the class I taught based on this quilt.

All the Luck of the Irish
by Helen Marshall, 35" x 35"

I altered the Wheel of Mystery template to make a trefoil and create a cloverleaf. The Irish theme continues with Nine Patch blocks arranged into an Irish Chain pattern, and with shamrocks free-motion quilted into the background. This time the blocks are set straight.

Consolation Fish *by Helen Marshall, 30" x 38½"*

Inspiration for this quilt came from a consolation gift of fish-print fabric given to me by women in South Africa when I was unable to make a trip there due to family illness. The blocks are set on point. The lines made by the A and B pieces seem to form a fish shape. The quilt is embellished with three-dimensional fabric shells and seaweed.

Midnight Waratahs *by Lorraine Bradley, 47" x 47"*

This quilt is another version of "Tropical Flowers of the Night" (page 32).
Using one color for the background makes the blocks appear to float.

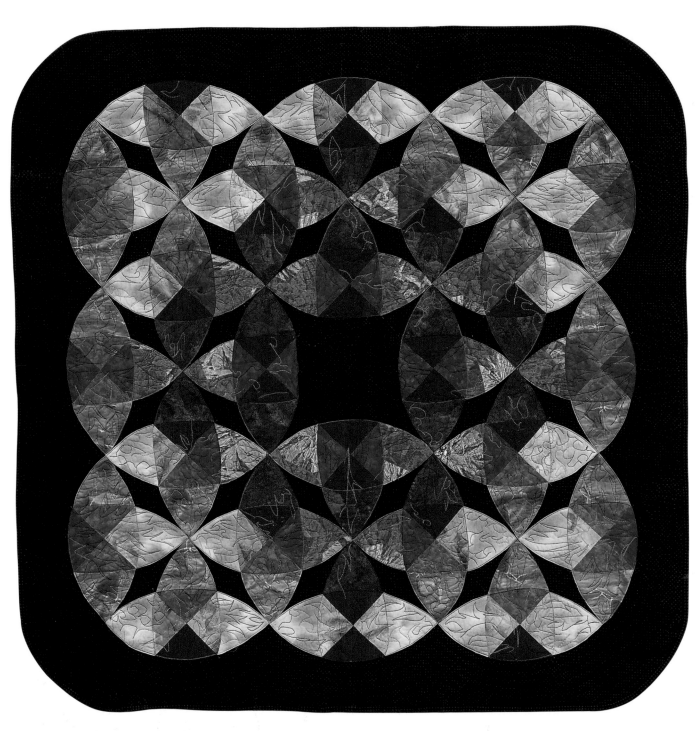

Rims of Fire *by Timothe Mansfield, 39" x 39"*

Timothe created an explosive design with her choice of fabric colors. With a black square for the quilt center and background, this quilt takes on a totally different feel than its inspiration, "Floating Circles" (page 33).

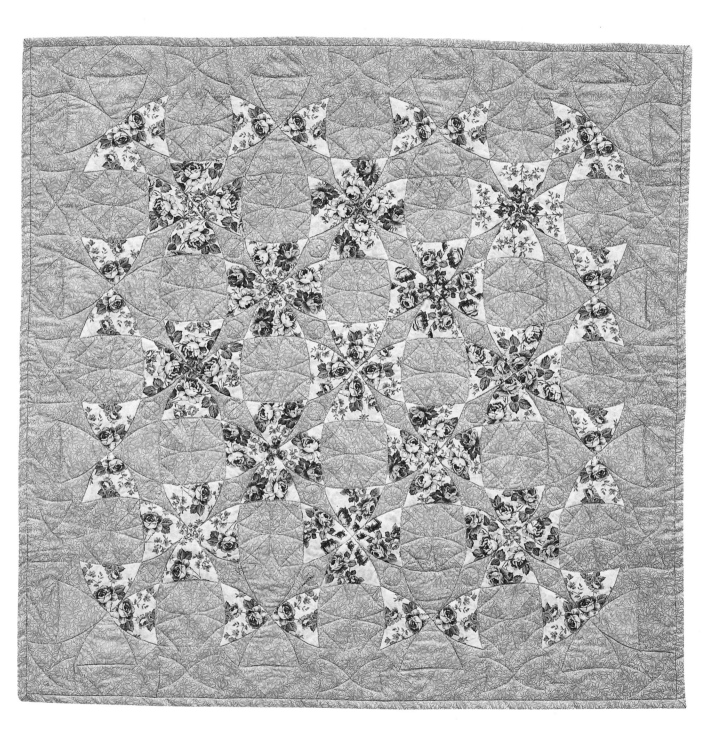

A Pocket Full of Posies *by Timothe Mansfield, 39" x 39"*

Although this quilt is the same pattern as "Midnight Waratahs" (page 35),
using a light background fabric produces a different look.

Where Has My Sarong Gone? *by Lindsey Blaymires, 40" x 40"*

Like "Midnight Waratahs" (page 35) and "A Pocket Full of Posies" (page 37), this pattern is created with full and half blocks set on point. The border, however, is created from the same fabrics used for the blocks rather than the background fabric.

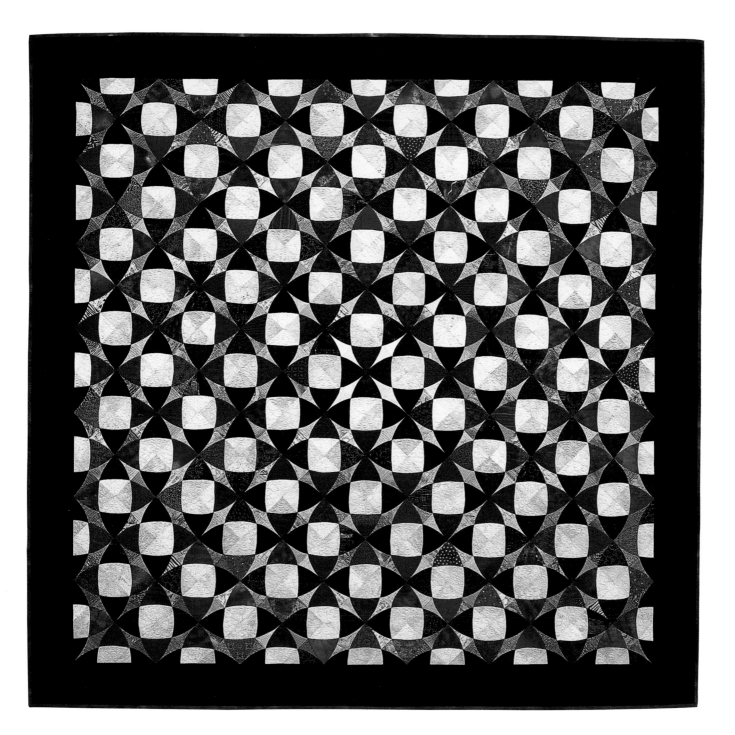

Circulation *by Chris Kenna, 78"x 78"*

Chris Kenna was keen to make a quilt for the book and started to make this quilt using the "Tropical Flowers of the Night" pattern (page 32). It grew somewhat!

At Liberty to Wander *by Marge Hurst, 28" x 28"*

Marge made this quilt with 4" blocks using Liberty fabrics. It is hand pieced, using a larger version of the "Tropical Flowers of the Night" (page 32) pattern, and then hand quilted.

Fruit Cobbler Picnic Cloth *by Helen Marshall, 39" x 39"*

Following along with the theme of "Down Under Christmas" at left, I used the realistic fruit-print fabric to make a summer picnic cloth, arranging the whole and partial blocks so that they resembled fruit cobbler desserts. This arrangement was also used in "Oh for a Scarlet Hat" (page 55). The fruit was outline quilted and the background was quilted with a grid pattern.

Down Under Christmas *by Helen Marshall, 19" x 57"*

I am in a quilting group that has annual "challenge" projects; one year, the challenge was to make a Christmas quilt. Because Christmas is during the summer in New Zealand, I immediately thought of using the strawberry-print and grape-print fabrics for a real "Down Under" Christmas. I used the golden fabric to offset the red and green and to form a star shape for the quilt. The quilting outlines the fruit. I used whole and partial blocks like I did in "Oh for a Scarlet Hat" (page 55) and set them on point.

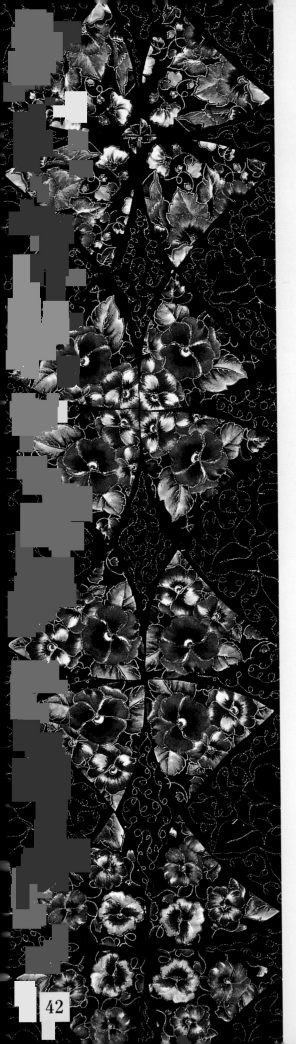

Pansy Posies

I love the cheeky faces of pansies and I always plant them in my garden. Every April, when the new seedlings come into the garden center, the big decision I have to make is what combination of colors to plant this year. The pansy fabric in this quilt has been a favorite of mine for a long time, and I was so pleased when it was reprinted.

Fabric Selection

For the template A pieces, choose a pansy fabric with several different groupings of flowers, ideally with small and large bunches. The size of the flowers should range from 1" to 1½" in diameter. The A pieces will be fussy cut to make wheels of flowers in different arrangements. Try not to cut the flowers up too much—have some whole flowers in each patch.

For the background, use a solid or tone-on-tone fabric that matches the background of the pansy fabric and allows the flowers to stand out. I chose a black solid.

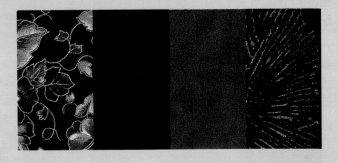

Pieced and quilted by Helen Marshall, 33" x 33"

MATERIALS

Yardages are based on 42"-wide fabrics.

2 yards of pansy print for blocks*

2 yards of solid or tone-on-tone fabric for blocks and border

¼ yard of fabric for piping

⅜ yard of fabric for binding

1¼ yards of fabric for backing

39" x 39" piece of batting

4 yards of thin cord or string for piping

6" x 10" piece of heavyweight cardboard for block templates

6" x 6" piece of lightweight cardboard for window template

Yardage is approximate and will vary depending on the pattern repeat and the motifs you want to use. To determine the actual yardage needed, refer to "Fussy Cutting" (page 15).

CUTTING

Before you begin cutting, follow the instructions in "Making the Templates" (page 14) to make templates A, B, and C from heavyweight cardboard. You will also need to make a window template for A to fussy cut the desired motifs from the pansy fabric. Refer to "Fussy Cutting" (page 15). All measurements include ¼"-wide seam allowances.

From the pansy print, cut:

‡ 16 sets of 4 fussy-cut template A pieces (64 total). The pieces in each set should be identical, but there should be some variety between sets.

From the solid or tone-on-tone fabric, cut:

‡ 2 strips, 3" x 30", along the lengthwise grain

‡ 2 strips, 3" x 38", along the lengthwise grain

‡ 64 template B pieces

‡ 64 template C pieces

From the piping fabric, cut:

‡ 4 strips, 1½" x 42"

From the binding fabric, cut:

‡ 4 strips, 2" x 42"

MAKING THE BLOCKS AND ASSEMBLING THE QUILT TOP

1. Refer to "Wheel of Mystery Block Construction" (page 18) to make 16 blocks using the A, B, and C pieces. The A pieces should match in each block. Because the pieces are not always cut along the grain line, be careful that you don't distort the edges when you press. If necessary, square up the blocks so they measure 7½" x 7½", being careful not to cut off any of the points.

Make 16.

2. Arrange the blocks into four horizontal rows of four blocks each on your design wall. Rearrange the blocks until you are satisfied with the layout. Label each block with its row and position using a numbered self-adhesive dot. A digital picture of the block arrangement is also helpful.

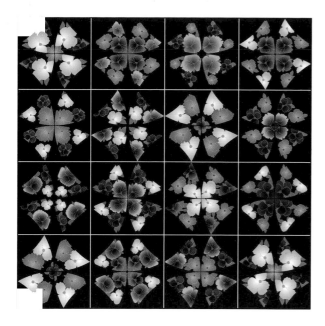

3. Sew the blocks in each row together. Press the seams open. Sew the rows together, sewing each row from the opposite direction as the previous row to prevent distortion. Press the seams open.

4. Measure the quilt top from side to side through the horizontal center. Trim the 3" x 30" solid or tone-on-tone strips to the length measured. Sew the trimmed strips to the top and bottom edges of the quilt top. Press the seams toward the borders.

5. Measure the quilt top from top to bottom through the vertical center. Trim the 3" x 38" solid or tone-on-tone strips to the length measured. Sew the trimmed strips to the sides of the quilt top. Press the seams toward the borders.

FINISHING

Refer to "Finishing Techniques" (page 22) as needed for assistance with any of the following steps.

1. Cut the backing fabric so it measures 6" longer and 6" wider than the quilt top.

2. Layer the quilt top with batting and backing; baste.

3. Quilt as desired. I stabilized the quilt by machine stitching 1/8" from the A pieces with black thread. I free-motion stitched a small design of pansies and leaves on the B pieces with gold thread. To do this, I traced the design onto pieces of water-soluble material with a water-soluble pen that wasn't the same color as the background fabric and then cut out the design, leaving a 1/4" margin. The design was then pinned into place and stitched. After pulling away the majority of the water-soluble material, I filled in the rest of the background with a tiny loop pattern and then sprayed the quilt with water to remove any remaining water-soluble material.

Note: If you pressed your seams open, *do not* stitch in the ditch. You'll only be stitching over thread since there is no seam allowance under the seam.

Quilting detail

4. Block the quilt and let it dry. Trim away the excess batting and backing.

5. Refer to "Piping" (page 25) to cover the cord or string with the piping-fabric strips and apply it to the edges of the border.

6. Bind the quilt edges with the binding-fabric strips.

7. Make a hanging sleeve, if desired, and stitch it to the backing.

8. Add a label and sign your quilt.

Passion Fruit

I adore passion fruit for its flamboyant flowers, flavor, and colors. We have several vines growing in the garden and the colors of the fruit inspired this quilt. When the fruit is cut, the deep plum color of the wrinkled skin reveals the inside color combination of yellow and orange. I wanted to make a quilt in a complementary color scheme and chose the colors of this fruit as the basis. The lime green and the bright blue used for the inner border suggest leaves and sky.

Fabric Selection

"Passion Fruit" uses a narrow color scheme. The color groups I used were purple/burgundy and yellow/orange with accents of green and blue in a combination of batik, hand-dyed, and tone-on-tone fabrics.

Pieced by Helen Marshall, 43" x 57". Quilted by Bary Scott.

MATERIALS

Yardages are based on 42"-wide fabrics.

1⅞ yards of burgundy batik fabric for blocks, outer border, and binding

1⅛ yards *total* of assorted burgundy, plum, and purple tone-on-tone, hand-dyed, and/or batik fabrics for blocks

⅝ yard of light purple batik fabric for blocks

⅝ yard *total* of assorted medium yellow tone-on-tone, hand-dyed, and/or batik fabrics for blocks

⅝ yard *total* of assorted light yellow tone-on-tone, hand-dyed, and/or batik fabrics for blocks

½ yard *total* of assorted medium orange tone-on-tone, hand-dyed, and/or batik fabrics for blocks

⅜ yard *total* of assorted bright blue tone-on-tone, hand-dyed, and/or batik fabrics for blocks

⅜ yard *total* of assorted lime green tone-on-tone, hand-dyed, and/or batik fabrics for blocks

¼ yard of bright blue fabric for inner border

¼ yard of lime green fabric for inner border

3⅜ yards of fabric for backing

49" x 63" piece of batting

6" x 10" piece of heavyweight cardboard for block templates

CUTTING

Before you begin cutting, follow the instructions in "Making the Templates" (page 14) to make templates A, B, and C from heavyweight cardboard. All measurements include ¼"-wide seam allowances.

From the burgundy batik fabric, cut:

- ⚜ 2 strips, 4" x 38", along the lengthwise grain
- ⚜ 2 strips, 4" x 59", along the lengthwise grain
- ⚜ 4 strips, 3" x 59", along the lengthwise grain
- ⚜ 16 template A pieces
- ⚜ 16 template B pieces

From the assorted burgundy, plum, and purple fabrics, cut a *total* of:

- ⚜ 56 template A pieces
- ⚜ 54 template B pieces

From the assorted medium orange fabrics, cut a *total* of:

- ⚜ 72 template C pieces

From the assorted medium yellow fabrics and the remaining medium orange fabrics, cut a *total* of:

- ⚜ 70 template B pieces

From the light purple batik fabric, cut:

- ⚜ 34 template A pieces

From the assorted light yellow fabrics, cut a *total* of:

- ⚜ 34 template A pieces

From the assorted bright blue fabrics for blocks, cut a *total* of:

- ⚜ 34 template C pieces

From the assorted lime green fabrics for blocks, cut a *total* of:

- ⚜ 34 template C pieces

From the bright blue fabric for inner border, cut:

- ⚜ 1 strip, 1" x 37"
- ⚜ 2 strips, 1" x 42"

From the lime green fabric for inner border, cut:

- ⚜ 1 strip, 1" x 37"
- ⚜ 2 strips, 1" x 42"

MAKING THE BLOCKS

1. Select four assorted burgundy, plum, or purple template A pieces; two assorted burgundy, plum, or purple template B pieces; two assorted

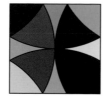

medium yellow or medium orange template B pieces; and four assorted medium orange template C pieces. Arrange and pin these pieces to your design wall as shown to make a dark block.

Dark block

2. Select two light purple batik template A pieces; two light yellow template A pieces; two assorted burgundy, plum, or purple template B pieces; two assorted medium yellow or medium orange template B pieces; two assorted bright blue template C pieces; and two assorted lime green template C pieces. Arrange and pin these pieces to your design wall next to the dark block as shown to make a light block.

Light block

3. Continue to arrange the pieces for the dark and light blocks into seven horizontal rows of five blocks each as shown, alternating the dark and light blocks in each row and from row to row. Try and arrange the pieces so that adjoining fabrics from the same color group are different. Be sure the blue and green patches are in the correct positions.

4. When you are satisfied with the arrangement of all of the pieces, label the top left-hand A piece of each block with a numbered self-adhesive dot. A digital picture of the block arrangement is also helpful.

5. Refer to "Wheel of Mystery Block Construction" (page 18) to sew the block pieces together. To keep the blocks in the correct order, make one block at a time and replace it on the design wall before removing the pieces for the next block. If necessary, square up the blocks so they measure 7½" x 7½", being careful not to cut off any of the points.

6. Double-check to make sure all of the blocks are arranged on the design wall correctly.

ASSEMBLING THE QUILT TOP

1. Sew the blocks in each row together. Press the seams open. Sew the rows together, sewing each row from the opposite direction as the previous row to prevent distortion. Press the seams open.

2. Measure the quilt top from side to side through the horizontal center. Trim the 1" x 37" bright blue strips and lime green strips to the length measured. Sew the bright blue strip to the top edge of the quilt top and the lime green strip to the bottom edge of the quilt top. Press the seams toward the borders.

3. Join the 1" x 42" bright blue strips end to end to make one long strip. Repeat with the 1" x 42" lime green strips. Measure the quilt top from top to bottom through the vertical center. Trim the pieced strips to the length measured. Sew the trimmed bright blue strip to the right-hand side of the quilt top and the trimmed lime green strip to the left-hand side of the quilt top. Press the seams toward the borders.

4. Measure the quilt top from side to side through the horizontal center. Trim the 4" x 38" burgundy batik strips to the length measured. Sew the trimmed strips to the top and bottom edges of the quilt top. Press the seams toward the inner borders.

5. Measure the quilt top from top to bottom through the vertical center. Trim the 4" x 59" burgundy batik strips to the length measured. Sew the trimmed strips to the top and bottom edges of the quilt top. Press the seams toward the inner borders.

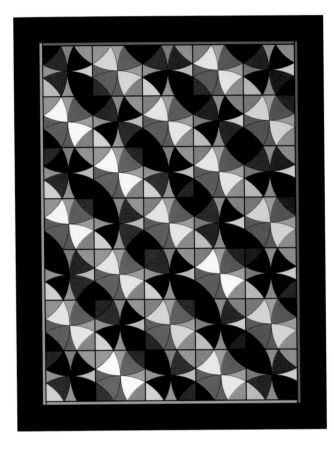

FINISHING

Refer to "Finishing Techniques" (page 22) as needed for assistance with any of the following steps.

1. Piece and cut the backing fabric so it measures 6" longer and 6" wider than the quilt top.

2. Layer the quilt top with batting and backing; baste.

3. Quilt as desired. For this quilt, I used a passion fruit theme. A pair of leaves and tendrils were quilted in a matching thread throughout the yellow portion of the quilt. This design was repeated in the purple sections with extra tendrils on the adjoining purple A pieces of the light blocks. The border was quilted with a continuous pattern of leaves and tendrils.

Note: If you pressed your seams open, *do not* stitch in the ditch. You'll only be stitching over thread since there is no seam allowance under the seam.

Quilting detail

4. Block the quilt and let it dry. Trim away the excess batting and backing.

5. Bind the quilt edges with the burgundy batik strips.

6. Make a hanging sleeve, if desired, and stitch it to the backing.

7. Add a label and sign your quilt.

Sunday in the Pacific

The inspiration for this quilt came from the beautiful flower-decorated hats the ladies in the Pacific Islands wear to church. When viewed from above, the sea of hats with beautiful flowers melds with the darkness of the furniture and begs to be translated into fabric.

Fabric Selection

Choose light-colored miniature prints with textures that mimic straw hats for the hats. The flowers will need to show up against this fabric, so look for pale colors.

Choose fabrics with a weave or lace-like print for the hats.

For the flowers, choose fabrics with a variety of brightly colored 1" to 1½" flowers. Each flower fabric should work well with at least one of the hat fabrics. Four fussy-cut B pieces will be cut from four different areas of each fabric (16 total). One piece from each area is used to form identical bouquets.

The flowers on these fabrics would work well.

The flowers on these fabrics are too big.

For the hair, I chose a black tone-on-tone fabric. I used a brown batik for the wood flooring and a dark brown mottled fabric for the shadows.

These fabrics would be suitable for the hair, floor, and shadows.

Pieced and quilted by Helen Marshall, 42" x 42"

MATERIALS

Yardages are based on 42"-wide fabrics.

½ yard *each* of 9 tropical floral prints on black backgrounds for hat flowers*

⅜ yard *each* of 9 light prints for hats

1¼ yards of brown tone-on-tone or batik fabric for floor and binding

½ yard of black tone-on-tone fabric for hair

⅜ yard of dark brown fabric for shadows

3 yards of fabric for backing

48" x 48" piece of batting

6" x 10" piece of heavyweight cardboard for block templates

6" x 6" piece of lightweight cardboard for window template

*Yardage is approximate and will vary depending on the pattern repeat and the motifs you want to use. To determine the actual yardage needed, refer to "Fussy Cutting" (page 15).

CUTTING

Before you begin cutting, follow the instructions in "Making the Templates" (page 14) to make templates A, B, and C from heavyweight cardboard. You will also need to make a window template for B to fussy cut the desired motifs from the hat flower fabrics. Refer to "Fussy Cutting" (page 15). All measurements include ¼"-wide seam allowances.

From *each* of the 9 light prints, cut:

⊞ 12 template A pieces (108 total). Match the fabric pattern if necessary.

From *each* of the 9 tropical floral prints, cut:

⊞ 4 sets of 4 fussy-cut template B pieces (144 total). The pieces in each set should be identical, but there should be some variety between sets.

From the brown tone-on-tone or batik fabric, cut:

⊞ 192" of 2"-wide bias strips

⊞ 32 template A pieces

From the black tone-on-tone fabric, cut:

⊞ 72 template C pieces

From the dark brown fabric, cut:

⊞ 48 template C pieces

MAKING THE BLOCKS

1. Separate the hat pieces (A) and the flower pieces (B) into nine groups. Each group should have all of the A pieces from one fabric and all of the B pieces from a fabric that complements the A fabric.

2. Refer to the illustration to pin the A pieces to your design wall first. Make sure there is sufficient contrast between adjacent hats. Add the B pieces you selected for each hat next. Arrange the bouquets so you use one of each of the four motifs in each bouquet and that identical motifs are in the same position in each bouquet. When you are satisfied with the combinations, fill in with the remaining A pieces and the C pieces.

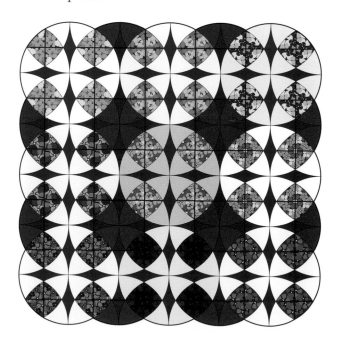

3. Refer to the illustration below (which shows a portion of the quilt top) to separate the pieces into rows. Whole blocks will make up the inside of the quilt top, with half blocks creating the scalloped edges and B pieces creating the corners. Label all of the pieces in each row with a numbered self-adhesive dot. A digital picture of the block arrangement is also helpful.

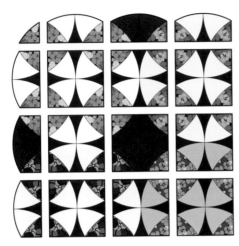

4. Refer to "Wheel of Mystery Block Construction" (page 18) to sew the block pieces together, following all of the steps to make the whole blocks and only steps 1–5 to make the half blocks. To keep the pieces in the correct order, make one block at a time and replace it on the design wall before removing the pieces for the next block. If necessary, square up the whole blocks so they measure 7½" x 7½" and the half blocks so they measure 7½" x 4".

5. Double-check to make sure all of the blocks are arranged on the design wall correctly.

ASSEMBLING THE QUILT TOP

Sew the blocks in each row together, adding the corner pieces to the ends of the top and bottom rows of half blocks. Press the seams open. Sew the rows together, sewing each row from the opposite direction as the previous row to prevent distortion. Press the seams open.

FINISHING

Refer to "Finishing Techniques" (page 22) as needed for assistance with any of the following steps.

1. Piece and cut the backing fabric so it measures 6" longer and 6" wider than the quilt top.

2. Layer the quilt top with batting and backing; baste.

3. Quilt as desired. I free-motion quilted the outline of each flower with matching thread. The floor and shadow fabrics were crosshatched with brown thread. Each hat was quilted with a different design and thread that matched the hat fabric. Sometimes the design followed the fabric pattern, and other times I used a built-in stitch on my machine.

Note: If you pressed your seams open, *do not* stitch in the ditch. You'll only be stitching over thread since there is no seam allowance under the seam.

Shadow quilting   *Hat quilting*

4. Block the quilt and let it dry. Trim away the excess batting and backing.

5. Bind the quilt edges with the brown bias strips.

6. Make a hanging sleeve, if desired, and stitch it to the backing.

7. Add a label and sign your quilt.

Oh for a Scarlet Hat

After I had finished "Sunday in the Pacific," *I decided to make a mini-quilt for all those people who enjoy the poem by Jenny Joseph about wearing purple with a red hat.*

Fabric Selection

Of course you'll need to use red fabric for the hat and purple fabric for the background. I chose tone-on-tone fabrics for both of these. To decorate the hat brim, select a print with red and purple flowers that range from 1" to 1½" in diameter. You'll be using this fabric for the three-dimensional flowers and leaves, as well as for the pieces under them. Silver or gray is a good choice for the hair.

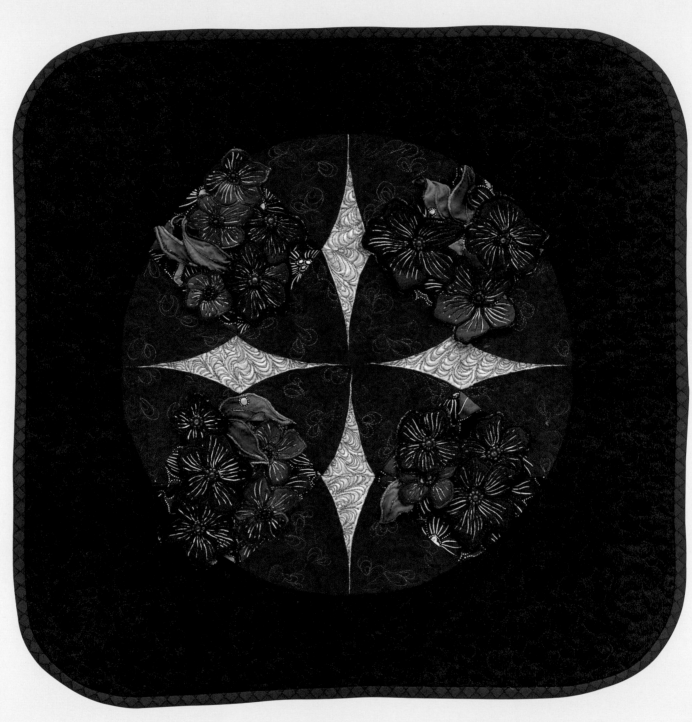

Pieced and quilted by Helen Marshall, 21" x 21"

MATERIALS

Yardages are based on 42"-wide fabrics.

⅝ yard of purple tone-on-tone fabric for background

½ yard of red tone-on-tone fabric for hat

½ yard of red-and-purple floral print for hat decorations and three-dimensional flowers

¼ yard of light gray print for hair

½ yard of red-and-purple checked fabric for binding

⅞ yard of fabric for backing of quilt

½ yard of fabric for backing of three-dimensional flowers

27" x 27" piece of batting for quilt

12" x 12" piece of high-loft batting for three-dimensional flowers

11" x 14" piece of heavyweight cardboard for block templates

Purple and green rayon or cotton machine-embroidery thread

½ yard of water-soluble stabilizer

15 to 20 beads for three-dimensional-flower centers (the exact amount will depend on the amount of flowers you make)

8"-diameter embroidery hoop

Machine-embroidery needle

Presser feet: open-toe free-motion; open-toe embroidery

CUTTING

Before you begin cutting, follow the instructions in "Making the Templates" (page 14) to make templates A, B, C, E, and F. All measurements include ¼"-wide seam allowances.

From the red tone-on-tone fabric, cut:

✤ 12 template A pieces

From the red-and-purple floral print, cut:

✤ 16 template B pieces. Set the remainder aside for the three-dimensional flowers.

From the light gray print, cut:

✤ 8 template C pieces

From the purple tone-on-tone fabric, cut:

✤ 4 template E pieces
✤ 4 template F pieces

From the red-and-purple checked fabric, cut:

✤ 100" of 2"-wide bias strips (cut with scissors through the center of the checks)

MAKING THE BLOCKS

1. Refer to "Wheel of Mystery Block Construction" (page 18) to make block A using the template A, B, and C pieces. Make one.

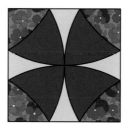

Block A.
Make 1.

2. Refer to steps 1–5 of "Wheel of Mystery Block Construction" to make a half block using the A, B, and C pieces. Stitch a template E piece to the curved edge as shown to make block B. Press the seam open. Make four.

Block B.
Make 4.

3. To make block C, sew a template F piece to one of the remaining template B pieces as shown. Press the seam open. Make four.

Block C.
Make 4.

4. If necessary, square up the A and B blocks so they measure 7½" x 7½", being careful not to cut off any of the points.

ASSEMBLING THE QUILT TOP

1. Arrange blocks A, B, and C into three horizontal rows of three blocks each as shown.

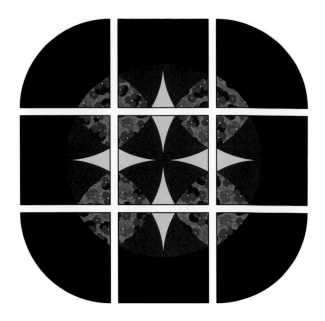

2. Sew the blocks in each row together. Press the seams open. Sew the rows together, sewing each row from the opposite direction as the previous row to prevent distortion. Press the seams open.

FINISHING

Refer to "Finishing Techniques" (page 22) as needed for assistance with any of the following steps.

1. Cut the quilt backing fabric so it measures 6" longer and 6" wider than the quilt top.

2. Layer the quilt top with batting and backing; baste.

3. Quilt as desired. I free-motion stitched around the outline of the flowers in the B pieces and stitched some wavy lines on the C pieces. The backing fabric was printed with different-sized circles, so I worked from the wrong side and quilted around these circles in the brim area, using the previous lines of stitching as a guide.

Note: If you pressed your seams open, *do not* stitch in the ditch. You'll only be stitching over thread since there is no seam allowance under the seam.

4. To make the three-dimensional flowers, cut out several clusters of two or three flowers and several individual flowers and leaves from the remaining floral fabric, leaving about ½" of excess fabric around each motif or cluster. Place the backing fabric in the hoop, wrong side up. Pin the 12" x 12" square of batting onto the backing. It will extend beyond the hoop. Pin as many flower pieces as you can to the batting within the hoop, leaving enough room to stitch around each one.

5. Thread your needle and bobbin with purple embroidery thread. If your bobbin case has a finger with an eye on it, insert the thread through the eye. Consult your sewing machine manual if necessary.

6. Drop the feed dogs and put the open-toe free-motion foot on your machine. Place the hoop under the needle. Straight stitch around the visible outer edges of each flower. Raise the feed dogs. Remove the free-motion presser foot and replace it with the open-toe embroidery foot. Set your machine for a narrow satin stitch (the same setting as for buttonholes). Stitch over the straight stitching, moving the hoop as necessary.

7. Remove the hoop from under the machine. Use sharp scissors to trim close to the outside edges of the satin stitching around each flower.

8. Rehoop the backing fabric and repeat if necessary for any remaining flowers.

9. Hoop the water-soluble stabilizer and pin as many trimmed flowers as you can to the stabilizer within the hoop, leaving enough room to stitch around each one. Adjust the width of the satin stitch so it is slightly wider than the previous satin stitching. Using the open-toe embroidery foot, stitch around each motif, covering the previous satin stitching. Drop the feed dogs, attach the open-toe free-motion foot, and set the machine for a straight stitch. Stitch over the inner petal lines and around the center of each flower. Cut the pieces away from the stabilizer. Rehoop the stabilizer and repeat for any remaining flowers.

10. Follow the manufacturer's instructions to remove the stabilizer from the flowers.

11. Repeat the process with the leaf motifs using green embroidery thread and no batting or backing.

12. Arrange the flower clusters, individual flowers, and leaves over the B pieces as desired. Tack the pieces in place, leaving the edges free. Sew a bead or cluster of beads to the center of each flower.

13. Block the quilt and let it dry. Trim away the excess batting and backing.

14. Bind the quilt edges with the checked strips.

15. Make a hanging sleeve, if desired, and stitch it to the backing.

16. Add a label and sign your quilt.

Japanese Fans

 *This quilt is a smaller version of "Lordy, Miss Claudie, It's Gaudy!" (page 31). I already had several Japanese fabrics in my stash that went well together, and I chose the red and navy blue fabrics to feature in this quilt. The navy blue fabrics are used in both the A and B pieces of the blue blocks to give them a different look. The red fabrics are used for the whole blocks in the center of the quilt and for the partial blocks along the border.*

Fabric Selection

I chose five different Japanese prints, three with a navy background and two with a red background, to use for the fussy-cut A pieces and some of the B pieces. Fussy-cut pieces are cut to feature a motif from the printed fabric in the center of the piece. Each set of pieces features a different motif. A pale yellow batik was used for the background, and I chose a navy tone-on-tone print for the outer border. The border is added in one piece, and the excess is removed after the patchwork is attached.

Pieced by Helen Marshall, 34" x 44". Quilted by Bary Scott.

MATERIALS

Yardages are based on 42"-wide fabrics.

2 yards of dark blue fabric for border and binding

½ yard *each* of 3 navy Japanese prints for blocks*

½ yard *each* of 2 red Japanese prints for blocks*

¾ yard of light yellow batik fabric for background

1⅝ yards of fabric for backing

40" x 50" piece of batting

6" x 10" piece of heavyweight cardboard for block templates

6" x 10" piece of lightweight cardboard for window templates

*Yardage is approximate and will vary depending on the pattern repeat and the motifs you want to use. To determine the actual yardage needed, refer to "Fussy Cutting" (page 15).

CUTTING

Before you begin cutting, follow the instructions in "Making the Templates" (page 14) to make templates A, B, and C from heavyweight cardboard. You will also need to make window templates for A and B to fussy cut the desired motifs from the indicated fabrics. Refer to "Fussy Cutting" (page 15). All measurements include ¼"-wide seam allowances.

From *each* of the 3 navy Japanese prints, cut:

⊞ 2 sets of 4 fussy-cut template A pieces (24 total). The pieces in each set should be identical, but there should be some variety between sets.

⊞ 2 sets of 4 fussy-cut template B pieces (24 total). The pieces in each set should be identical, but there should be some variety between sets.

From the light yellow batik fabric, cut:

⊞ 6 template A pieces

⊞ 44 template B pieces

⊞ 48 template C pieces

From *each* of the 2 red Japanese prints, cut:

⊞ 1 set of 4 fussy-cut template A pieces (8 total). The pieces should be identical.

⊞ 5 sets of 2 fussy-cut template A pieces (20 total). The pieces in each set should be identical, but there should be some variety between sets.

From the dark blue fabric, cut:

⊞ 1 rectangle, 34" x 44"

⊞ 5 strips, 3" x 42"

MAKING THE BLOCKS

1. Refer to "Wheel of Mystery Block Construction" (page 18) to make block A as shown. Use four identical navy A pieces, four identical navy B pieces, and four light yellow C pieces. Because the fussy-cut pieces are not always cut along the grain line, be careful that you don't distort the edges when you press. Make six. If necessary, square up the blocks so they measure 7½" x 7½", being careful not to cut off any of the points.

Block A.
Make 6.

2. Make block B as shown, using four identical red A pieces, four light yellow B pieces, and four light yellow C pieces. Make two.

Block B.
Make 2.

3. To make block C, follow steps 1–5 of "Wheel of Mystery Block Construction" to make a half block, using one red A piece, one light yellow A piece, two light yellow B pieces, and one light yellow C piece. Sew another light yellow C piece to the light yellow A piece as shown. Clip 1" from the wide end of the C piece. Press the seam in the same manner as the other C seams. Join the red A piece that matches the previous red A piece to a light yellow B piece. Press the seam open. Sew the two units together. Clip 1" from the wide end of the seam and press as you did for the previous C seams. Make six.

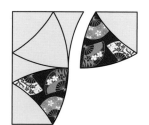

Block C.
Make 6.

4. Follow steps 1–5 of "Wheel of Mystery Block Construction" to make block D. Use two identical red A pieces, two light yellow B pieces, and one light yellow C piece. Make four.

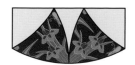

Block D.
Make 4.

ASSEMBLING THE QUILT TOP

1. Arrange the blocks and the remaining light yellow B pieces on your design wall as shown.

2. When you are satisfied with the arrangement, separate the blocks and B pieces into diagonal rows as shown. Label each block with its row and position using a numbered self-adhesive dot. A digital picture of the block arrangement is also helpful.

3. Sew the blocks in each diagonal row together, adding the B pieces to the ends of the rows where needed. Press the seams open. Sew the rows together, sewing each row from the opposite direction as the previous row to prevent distortion. Press the seams open.

4. Turn under the ¼" seam allowance on the edges of all of the outside pieces and baste them in place. Press.

5. Lay the rectangle of dark blue fabric on a large, flat surface and tape it in place. Center the joined blocks on the rectangle and pin in place through the center as well as along the outside edges of the blocks. Baste the pieces together along the block edges. Remove the tape.

6. Edge stitch the block piece to the border rectangle with matching thread. I used red thread for the red sections and yellow thread for the yellow sections.

7. Turn the quilt top to the wrong side. Cut away the border fabric under the blocks, leaving a ¼" seam allowance. Remove the basting stitches.

FINISHING

Refer to "Finishing Techniques" (page 22) as needed for assistance with any of the following steps.

1. Piece and cut the backing fabric so it measures 6" longer and 6" wider than the quilt top.

2. Layer the quilt top with batting and backing; baste.

3. Quilt as desired. In this quilt, the background spaces were quilted with fans using matching thread. The navy and red pieces were quilted ¼" inside the seam line. The smaller areas of the background were quilted in a meandering pattern. A random cloud pattern was stitched in the border.

    Note: If you pressed your seams open, *do not* stitch in the ditch. You'll only be stitching over thread since there is no seam allowance under the seam.

Quilting detail

4. Block the quilt and let it dry. Trim away the excess batting and backing.

5. Bind the quilt edges with the dark blue strips.

6. Make a hanging sleeve, if desired, and stitch it to the backing.

7. Add a label and sign your quilt.

Aloha

 Tropical sunsets truly are some of nature's most spectacular creations. With its beautiful flowers backed by sunset colors and surrounded by lush greenery, this quilt will give you a taste of the islands you'll soon want to enjoy in person.

Fabric Selection

You'll need several tropical flower prints with 3"- to 4"-diameter flowers on black backgrounds for the fussy-cut template A pieces. Some of the fabrics I began with needed a boost of color, so I used my fabric pens to enhance them.

Original fabrics (top) and the same pieces enhanced with fabric pens (bottom)

You can achieve lots of different effects with the flowers depending on how you position the motif. I found that the most pleasing arrangement came when the flowers were positioned slightly off center. Try to avoid centering a motif or using multiple flowers in each piece.

Cutting flower motifs off center, as shown, breaks up the original design and results in interesting new blossoms.

Centering motifs within piece A results in less compelling flowers.

Featuring multiple blossoms within piece A diminishes the impact of the final flower.

Pieced and quilted by Helen Marshall, 51" x 51"

The block B and C pieces are cut from many batiks and hand-dyed fabrics in sunset colors. I started with a sunset-striped batik and added single-color batiks that matched the colors in it. In order for the flowers to stand out, choose colors in the light range. Notice in the quilt photo how the background colors subtly flow from blues at the top of the quilt, to bluish yellow, and finally to hot pinks and peaches at the bottom, just like a tropical sky at sunset.

A tropical-sunset color range

The sashing is made up of several tropical leaf prints printed on black backgrounds. The strips are added to each block log-cabin style, which creates a double sashing. In order for each sashing strip to remain distinct and not blend into the next one, it's necessary to have a minimum of ten different fabrics. These prints are also used for the setting triangles that frame the quilt. Check your floral fabrics to see if there is an area of leafy print long enough to be used.

MATERIALS

Yardages are based on 42"-wide fabrics.

1 yard *each* of 6 to 8 tropical floral prints (with a variety of 3"- to 4"-diameter flowers on black backgrounds) for blocks*

⅓ yard *each* of at least 10 tropical leaf prints on black backgrounds for sashing and setting triangles

2½ yards *total* of assorted sunset-colored fabrics for block backgrounds

⅝ yard of tropical leaf print for binding (can be the same as one of the sashing prints)

3¼ yards of fabric for backing

57" x 57" piece of batting

6" x 10" piece of heavyweight cardboard for block templates

6" x 6" piece of lightweight cardboard for window template

Yardage is approximate and will vary depending on the pattern repeat and the motifs you want to use. To determine the actual yardage needed, refer to "Fussy Cutting" (page 15).

CUTTING

Before you begin cutting, follow the instructions in "Making the Templates" (page 14) to make templates A, B, and C from heavyweight cardboard. You will also need to make a window template for A to fussy cut the desired motifs from the tropical flower prints. Refer to "Fussy Cutting" (page 15). All measurements include ¼"-wide seam allowances.

From the 10 tropical leaf prints on black backgrounds for sashing and setting triangles, cut a *total* of:

✤ 100 strips, 1½" x 8½"

✤ 28 strips, 1½" x 10"

✤ 3 squares, 8" x 8"; cut each square twice diagonally to yield 12 side setting triangles

✤ 2 squares, 5¾" x 5¾"; cut each square once diagonally to yield 4 corner setting triangles

(Continued on page 68)

From the 6 to 8 tropical floral prints, cut a *total* of:

❖ 25 sets of 4 fussy-cut template A pieces. The pieces in each set should be identical.

From the tropical leaf print for binding, cut:

❖ 6 strips, 3" x 42"

PLANNING AND CUTTING THE BLOCK-BACKGROUND PIECES

Before you cut the background pieces, you'll need to audition the sunset-colored fabrics for placement to get a good color flow throughout the quilt. I suggest you make a color chart by cutting fabric swatches and taping them to a piece of paper in the order that you want the colors to flow.

In the illustration below, you can see that the top B and C pieces in a block are the same as the row above it. The bottom B piece is similar to the top pieces in the row below it. The side pieces can be the same as the top or bottom B pieces. The color does not need to match exactly between rows because the sashing interrupts the flow. However, when you stand back and look at the entire quilt, the colors should gradually change from one to another so the effect isn't jarring.

The quilt blocks are set on point. That means that the color changes of the sunset pattern need to run diagonally across the pieces so they will run horizontally when the blocks are placed on point. Half the B and C patches are cut with the design lines running one way and the other half with the design lines running the other way. Once you have determined the flow of color, cut out the B and C pieces from the desired fabrics as shown. If you're using batiks, you can use both the right and the wrong side of the fabrics. If you're using prints, you can only use the right side. In both cases you'll need to be careful about the placement of the template.

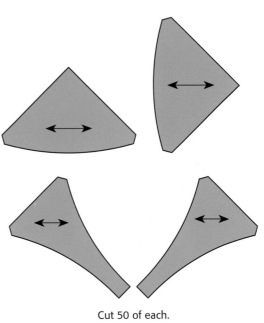

Cut 50 of each.

ARRANGING THE QUILT-TOP PIECES

1. Randomly select and pin the 1½" x 8½" tropical leaf print strips to your design wall as shown at the top of the facing page. Try not to have a print next to an identical print. Pin the 1½" x 10" strips around the outer edges. They will be longer than needed at this point.

3. When you are satisfied with the arrangement of all the pieces, label the uppermost A piece of each block with a numbered self-adhesive dot. A digital picture of the block arrangement is also helpful.

MAKING THE BLOCKS AND SETTING PIECES

1. Refer to "Wheel of Mystery Block Construction" (page 18) to sew the A, B, and C pieces together to make the Wheel of Mystery blocks. To keep the blocks in the correct order, make one block at a time and replace it on the design wall before removing the pieces for the next block. If necessary, square up the blocks so they measure 7½" x 7½", being careful not to cut off any of the points.

2. Double-check to make sure all of the units are arranged on the design wall correctly.

2. Add the B and C pieces to the design wall. When you are satisfied with the flow of color, add the A pieces. Use four identical A pieces for each block and make sure the flowers contrast with the background. You can check this by using a reducing glass, a camera viewfinder, or the "wrong" end of a pair of binoculars to get an overall view of the project. Rearrange the placement of the A pieces as needed to mix the shapes of the flower motifs as well as the colors. Add the side and corner setting triangles last.

3. Remove a Wheel of Mystery block along with the four single sashing strips on all sides, keeping them in the same order as they were on the design wall. With the end of the strip aligned with the top of the unit, sew the top right-hand strip to the unit, stopping 2" from the corner. Press the seam toward the sashing strip.

4. Sew the top left-hand strip to the unit and previous sashing strip as shown. Press the seam toward the sashing strip.

5. Continue working counterclockwise around the block to add the bottom strips in the same manner.

6. Finish sewing the first strip to the unit and sashing edges. The block should now measure 9½" x 9½". Pin the block back in place on the design wall.

7. Repeat steps 3–6 to make the remaining blocks.

8. To make each side setting triangle, remove the triangle and the two sashing strips next to it from the design wall. Position the triangle as shown. Align one end of the right-hand sashing strip with the point of the triangle. The opposite end will extend beyond the triangle. Sew the strip in place. Stitch the remaining strip to the left edge of the triangle as shown. Trim the ends of the strip so they are even with the long edge of the triangle. Sew one side setting triangle at a time and replace it on the design wall when you are finished.

9. To make each corner setting triangle, remove the triangle and the sashing strip next to it from the design wall. Center the strip on the triangle's long edge and stitch it in place. Trim the ends even with the short edges of the triangle. Sew one corner setting triangle at a time and replace it on the design wall when you are finished.

10. Double-check to make sure all of the blocks and setting pieces are arranged on the design wall correctly.

ASSEMBLING THE QUILT TOP

1. Separate the blocks and setting triangles into diagonal rows as shown.

2. Sew the blocks and side setting triangles in each row together. Press the seams open. Sew the rows together, sewing each row from the opposite direction as the previous row to prevent distortion. Press the seams open. Add the corner triangles last. Press the seams open.

FINISHING

Refer to "Finishing Techniques" (page 22) as needed for assistance with any of the following steps.

1. Piece and cut the backing fabric so it measures 6" longer and 6" wider than the quilt top.

2. Layer the quilt top with batting and backing; baste.

3. Quilt as desired. I did not want diagonal lines to show on the quilt, so I used water-soluble thread to stitch along the sides of the sashing first to stabilize the quilt. I then changed to green machine-embroidery thread and stitched a leaf motif through the center of all the sashing pieces and setting triangles. For the centers of the flowers, I added a few lines in a thread color that matched the main color of the flower. A small meandering pattern of leaves and stems was quilted on the sunset fabric with matching threads.

Note: If you pressed your seams open, *do not* stitch in the ditch. You'll only be stitching over thread since there is no seam allowance under the seam.

Quilting detail

4. Block the quilt and let it dry. Trim away the excess batting and backing to ¼" beyond the quilt top.

5. Bind the quilt edges with the tropical leaf print strips.

6. Make a hanging sleeve, if desired, and stitch it to the backing.

7. Add a label and sign your quilt.

Blocks of Fun

When I was planning quilts for this book a friend remarked, "Have you thought of doing a quilt for children?" I combined Wheel of Mystery blocks with a zigzag sashing to create a tumbling-blocks effect. The illusion is easy to create with light, medium, and dark fabrics from the same color family, and the quilt is sure to be enjoyed by children of all ages.

Fabric Selection

The focal point of the quilt is the Wheel of Mystery blocks, while the sashing strips create the three-dimensional illusion. I chose many different children's novelty prints for the fussy-cut A pieces, but the design also would work well with floral prints for a keen gardener or sport-themed fabrics for an active teenager.

To achieve the effect of the tumbling blocks, you will need light, medium, and dark solid-colored fabrics from the same family to go with each set of fussy-cut pieces. The background pieces of the Wheel of Mystery blocks will use the light fabrics. The zigzag sashing creates the sides of the tumbling blocks. Use the dark fabrics for the left side and the medium fabrics for the right side of the tumbling blocks. When sewing, be very careful to be consistent with your placement of the medium and dark sashing pieces. To make cutting easier, plan which solid fabrics you will use with each novelty fabric. You will need to use some of the solid fabrics more than once.

For the inner border and binding, I chose a black-and-white checked fabric so there would be a break from the color, and so the viewer's eye would have a place to rest. The outer border was made from strips of the leftover solid-colored fabrics.

Pieced by Helen Marshall, 39" x 56¼". Quilted by Bary Scott.

MATERIALS

Yardages are based on 42"-wide fabrics.

½ yard *each* of 9 dark-colored solids for sashing pieces and outer border

½ yard *each* of 9 medium-colored solids (from the same color families as the dark-colored solids) for sashing pieces and outer border

1 fat quarter *each* of 9 light-colored solids (from the same color families as the dark- and medium-colored solids) for template B and C pieces

1¼ yards *total* of assorted novelty prints for template A pieces*

¾ yard of black-and-white checked fabric for inner border and binding

2¾ yards of fabric for backing

45" x 63" piece of batting

8" x 10" piece of heavyweight cardboard for block and sashing templates

6" x 6" piece of lightweight cardboard for window template

Yardage is approximate and will vary depending on the pattern repeat and the motifs you want to use. To determine the actual yardage needed, refer to "Fussy Cutting" (page 15). The pieces for each block do not have to be identical or from the same fabric, but they do need to be from fabrics with a similar color background.

CUTTING

Before you begin cutting, follow the instructions in "Making the Templates" (page 14) to make templates A, B, C, G, and G reversed from heavyweight cardboard. You will also need to make a window template for A to fussy cut the desired motifs from the novelty fabrics. Refer to "Fussy Cutting" (page 15). All measurements include ¼"-wide seam allowances.

From the assorted novelty prints, cut a *total* of:

- 13 sets of 4 fussy-cut template A pieces (52 total). The pieces in each set should be cut from fabrics with a similar color background.
- 8 sets of 3 fussy-cut template A pieces (24 total). The pieces in each set should be cut from fabrics with a similar color background.
- 4 sets of 2 fussy-cut template A pieces (8 total). The pieces in each set should be cut from fabrics with a similar color background.

From the 9 light-colored solids, cut a *total* of:

- 13 sets consisting of 4 template B pieces and 4 template C pieces. Cut each set from the same color. Each set should coordinate with one of the 13 sets of 4 novelty print template A pieces.
- 8 sets consisting of 3 template B pieces and 2 template C pieces. Cut each set from the same color. Each set should coordinate with one of the 8 sets of 3 novelty print template A pieces.
- 4 sets consisting of 2 template B pieces and 1 template C piece. Cut each set from the same color. Each set should coordinate with one of the 4 sets of 2 novelty print template A pieces.

From *each* of the 9 medium-colored solids, cut:

- 3 strips, 1½" x 18" (27 total). Set the remaining fabric aside for the template G pieces.

From *each* of the 9 dark-colored solids, cut:

- 3 strips, 1½" x 18" (27 total). Set the remaining fabric aside for the template G reversed pieces.

From the black-and-white checked fabric, cut:

- 5 strips, 1½" x 42", along the crosswise grain (cut with scissors and follow the pattern)
- 5 strips, 3" x 42", along the crosswise grain (cut with scissors and follow the pattern)

MAKING THE BLOCKS

1. Refer to "Wheel of Mystery Block Construction" (page 18) to make block A as shown. Use one set of four novelty print A pieces and four B and C pieces from the same light-colored solid. Make 13.

Block A.
Make 13.

2. To make block B, use one set of three novelty print A pieces and three B and two C pieces from the same light-colored solid. Follow steps 1–5 of "Wheel of Mystery Block Construction" to make a half block. Sew the remaining C piece to the curved edge of the A piece as shown. Clip 1" from the wide end of the C piece. Press the seam in the same manner as the other C seams. Join the remaining A piece to the remaining B piece as shown. Press the seam open. Sew the two units together. Clip 1" from the wide end of the seam and press as you did for the previous C seams. Make eight.

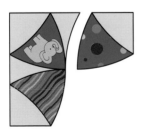 

Block B.
Make 8.

3. Follow steps 1–5 of "Wheel of Mystery Block Construction" to make block C. Use one set of two novelty print A pieces and two B pieces and one C piece from the same light-colored solid. Make four.

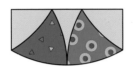

Block C.
Make 4.

ASSEMBLING THE QUILT TOP

1. Arrange the A, B, and C blocks on your design wall as shown, leaving room between the blocks for the G (sashing) pieces.

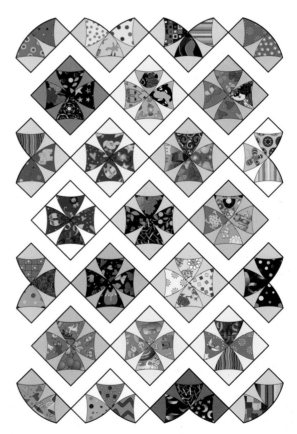

2. For each block A, cut one G piece from the remaining medium-colored solid that's in the same color family as the block background. Pin it to the open space on the lower-right edge of the block. Cut one G reversed piece from the remaining dark-colored solid that's also in the same color family. Pin it to the open space on the lower-left edge of the block. In the same manner, cut a G or G reversed piece for the lower edges of the B and C blocks. Blocks with an open space on the right side of the block need a medium G piece, while blocks with an open space on the left side of the block need a dark G reversed piece. Be sure the colors of the G pieces are from the same color family as the block backgrounds.

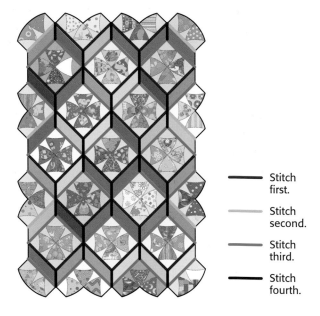

3. When you're satisfied with the arrangement of all the pieces, label each piece with its row and position using a numbered self-adhesive dot. A digital picture of the block arrangement is also helpful.

4. Refer to the illustration for the order in which to sew the sashing pieces to the blocks, beginning and ending your stitching ¼" from the points as indicated by the dots on the templates. Be careful not to catch previously sewn seams in adjacent seams. Press the seams toward the sashing pieces. Sew the sashing pieces together last. Press the seams open.

——— Stitch first.

——— Stitch second.

——— Stitch third.

——— Stitch fourth.

5. Use your rotary cutter and ruler to trim the extra fabric from the partial blocks on the sides, top, and bottom of the quilt top so the edges are straight, leaving a ¼" seam allowance beyond the block points as shown. The edges will be on the bias, so be careful not to stretch them.

6. Measure the quilt top from side to side through the horizontal center. Trim two of the 1½" x 42" black-and-white checked strips to the length measured. Sew the trimmed strips to the top and bottom edges of the quilt top. Press the seams toward the borders.

7. Join the remaining 1½" x 42" black-and-white checked strips end to end to make one long strip. Measure the quilt top from top to bottom through the vertical center. From the pieced strip, cut two strips to the length measured. Sew the trimmed strips to the sides of the quilt top. Press the seams toward the borders.

8. From the 1½" x 18" medium and dark-colored solid strips, randomly select 18 strips and sew them together along the long edges to make a strip set. Make three, arranging the colors differently in each set. Cut the strip sets into 12 segments, 4½" wide.

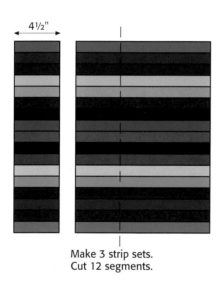

Make 3 strip sets.
Cut 12 segments.

9. Randomly join the segments together end to end to make one long strip. From the pieced strip, cut two 34" strips and two 60" strips.

10. Measure the quilt top from side to side through the horizontal center. Trim the 34" strips to the length measured and sew them to the top and bottom edges of the quilt top.

11. Measure the quilt top from top to bottom through the vertical center. Trim the 60" strips to the length measured and sew them to the top and bottom edges of the quilt top as shown above right.

FINISHING

Refer to "Finishing Techniques" (page 22) as needed for assistance with any of the following steps.

1. Piece and cut the backing fabric so it measures 6" longer and 6" wider than the quilt top.

2. Layer the quilt top with batting and backing; baste.

3. Quilt as desired. Because this quilt has so much visual interest and color, my quilter suggested that a large double-loop allover pattern done with a multicolored thread would be enough.

   Note: If you pressed your seams open, *do not* stitch in the ditch. You'll only be stitching over thread since there is no seam allowance under the seam.

4. Block the quilt and let it dry. Trim away the excess batting and backing.

5. Bind the quilt edges with the 3" x 42" black-and-white checked strips.

6. Make a hanging sleeve, if desired, and stitch it to the backing.

7. Add a label and sign your quilt.

Bali Lattice

This quilt is the result of pairing a secondary block with the Wheel of Mystery block. I modified the Flowering Snowball block by matching its seams to the seams of the Wheel of Mystery block so there would be a smooth flow across the quilt. By playing with the quilt's colors on my quilt-design software, I achieved the effect of two distinct layers in the quilt.

Fabric Selection

To achieve the layered look, you'll need to select a medium-value fabric for the background, two dark-value fabrics for the A pieces that form the wheels behind the lattice, and two medium-light-value fabrics for the lattice.

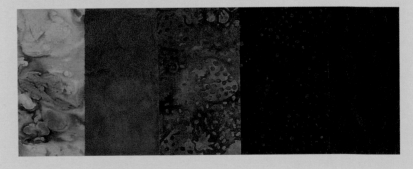

Pieced by Helen Marshall, 45" x 45". Quilted by Bary Scott.

MATERIALS

Yardages are based on 42"-wide fabrics.

2¼ yards of medium teal batik for the block backgrounds, border, and binding

¾ yard *each* of 2 medium-light pink batiks for the Flowering Snowball blocks (colors 3 and 4)

½ yard *each* of 2 dark purple batiks for the Wheel of Mystery blocks (colors 1 and 2)

3⅛ yards of fabric for backing

51" x 51" piece of batting

10" x 12" piece of heavyweight cardboard for block templates

CUTTING

Before you begin cutting, follow the instructions in "Making the Templates" (page 14) to make templates A, B, C, L, M, and N from heavyweight cardboard. All measurements include ¼"-wide seam allowances.

From *each* of the 2 dark purple batiks (colors 1 and 2), cut:
- 24 template A pieces (48 total)

From 1 medium-light pink batik (color 3), cut:
- 4 template L pieces
- 18 template N pieces
- 24 template B pieces

From the other medium-light pink batik (color 4), cut:
- 9 template L pieces
- 8 template N pieces
- 24 template B pieces

From the medium teal batik, cut:
- 3 strips, 3" x 72", along the lengthwise grain
- 2 strips, 5½" x 47", along the lengthwise grain
- 2 strips, 5½" x 37", along the lengthwise grain
- 48 template C pieces
- 52 template M pieces

MAKING THE BLOCKS

1. Refer to "Wheel of Mystery Block Construction" (page 18) to make 12 blocks as shown. For each block, use two color 1 template A pieces, two color 2 template A pieces, two color 3 template B pieces, two color 4 template B pieces, and four template C pieces. If necessary, square up the blocks so they measure 7½" x 7½", being careful not to cut off any of the points.

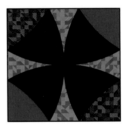

Make 12.

2. To make the Flowering Snowball I blocks, sew a template M piece to the curved edges of each color 4 template N piece as shown. Press the seams open. Sew two of these units to a color 3 template L piece. Press the seams open. Make four. Make the Flowering Snowball II blocks in the same manner using the template M pieces, the color 3 template N pieces, and the color

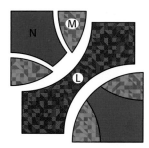

4 template L pieces. Make nine. If necessary, square up the blocks so they measure 7½" x 7½".

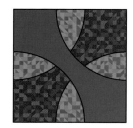

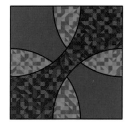

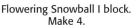

Flowering Snowball I block.
Make 4.

Flowering Snowball II block.
Make 9.

ASSEMBLING THE QUILT TOP

1. Arrange the blocks on your design wall as shown, paying careful attention to the placement and orientation of the Flowering Snowball blocks. Label the top-left corner of each block with its row and position using a numbered self-adhesive dot. A digital picture of the block arrangement is also helpful.

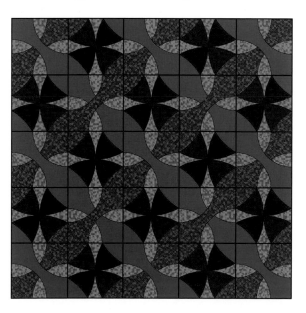

2. Sew the blocks in each row together. Press the seams open. Sew the rows together, sewing each row from the opposite direction as the previous row to prevent distortion. Press the seams open.

3. Measure the quilt top from side to side through the horizontal center. Trim the 5½" x 37" teal strips to the length measured. Sew the trimmed strips to the top and bottom edges of the quilt top. Press the seams toward the borders.

4. Measure the quilt top from top to bottom through the vertical center. Trim the 5½" x 47" teal strips to the length measured. Sew the trimmed strips to the sides of the quilt top. Press the seams toward the borders.

FINISHING

Refer to "Finishing Techniques" (page 22) as needed for assistance with any of the following steps.

1. Piece and cut the backing fabric so it measures 6" longer and 6" wider than the quilt top.

2. Layer the quilt top with batting and backing; baste.

3. Quilt as desired. For this quilt, my quilter stitched a medium-sized loop pattern on the lattice pieces. A small strawberry-leaf design was added to the A pieces. The border was quilted with strawberries and leaves to mimic the strawberry batik that was used for one of the lattices.

   Note: If you pressed your seams open, *do not* stitch in the ditch. You'll only be stitching over thread since there is no seam allowance under the seam.

4. Block the quilt and let it dry. Trim away the excess batting and backing.

5. Bind the quilt edges with the teal strips.

6. Make a hanging sleeve, if desired, and stitch it to the backing.

7. Add a label and sign your quilt.

Blue Ribbon

After a friend gave me a ribbon-striped fabric and some complementary fabrics, I decided to make a medallion quilt. The quilt is made up of the traditional Wheel of Mystery block in two color combinations; a variation of the block that uses only three A pieces, also in two color combinations; and two other blocks with diagonal pieces that create the woven-ribbon effect.

Fabric Selection

To create the ribbon effect, you'll need a border print or striped fabric that can be cut to 4¼" wide and finished to 3¾" wide. If you want to use a narrower stripe, you'll need to add a smaller strip to each side of the piece so it finishes to 3¾". The Wheel of Mystery blocks are made in two color combinations: one with dark wheels and a light-medium background fabric and the other with medium wheels and a white background. Select small-scale prints for all of the Wheel of Mystery block pieces.

Pieced by Helen Marshall, 49" x 49". Quilted by Bary Scott.

MATERIALS

Yardages are based on 42"-wide fabrics.

2 yards of light-medium small-scale print for block backgrounds

2 yards of white small-scale print for block backgrounds

1½ yards of border print or striped fabric with a 3¾"-wide pattern (that has ¼" of blank space on each side) for blocks E, F, and G*

1 yard of dark small-scale print for block A and C wheels

1 yard of medium small-scale print for block B and D wheels

⅝ yard of fabric for binding

3¼ yards of fabric for backing

55" x 55" piece of batting

10" x 20" piece of heavyweight cardboard for block templates

5" x 20" piece of lightweight cardboard for window template

*Yardage is approximate and will vary depending on the pattern repeat. To determine the actual yardage needed, refer to "Fussy Cutting" (page 15).

CUTTING

Before you begin cutting, follow the instructions in "Making the Templates" (page 14) to make templates A, B, C, D, H, J, J reversed, K, and K reversed. You will also need to make window templates for H and J to fussy cut the desired motifs from the striped fabric. Refer to "Fussy Cutting" (page 15). All measurements include ¼"-wide seam allowances.

From the dark small-scale print, cut:

+ 40 template A pieces

From the medium small-scale print for wheels, cut:

+ 40 template A pieces

From the light-medium small-scale print for block backgrounds, cut:

+ 40 template B pieces
+ 28 template C pieces
+ 12 template D pieces
+ 4 template K pieces
+ 4 template K reversed pieces
+ 8 squares, 5¼" x 5¼"; cut each square once diagonally to yield 16 triangles
+ 4 squares, 1¾" x 1¾"; cut each square once diagonally to yield 8 triangles

From the white small-scale print for block backgrounds, cut:

+ 40 template B pieces
+ 32 template C pieces
+ 8 template D pieces
+ 4 template K pieces
+ 4 template K reversed pieces
+ 8 squares, 5¼" x 5¼"; cut each square once diagonally to yield 16 triangles
+ 4 squares, 1¾" x 1¾"; cut each square once diagonally to yield 8 triangles

From the border print or striped fabric, cut:

+ 16 fussy-cut template H pieces. All pieces should be identical.
+ 8 fussy-cut template J pieces. All pieces should be identical.
+ 8 fussy-cut template J reversed pieces. All pieces should be identical.

From the binding fabric, cut:

+ 6 strips, 3" x 42"

MAKING THE BLOCKS

1. Refer to "Wheel of Mystery Block Construction" (page 18) to make blocks A and B as shown. For block A, use four dark A pieces and four *each* of the light-medium B and C pieces. Make one. For block B, use four medium A

pieces and four *each* of the white B and C pieces. Make four.

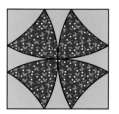

Block A.
Make 1.

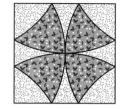

Block B.
Make 4.

2. To make block C, follow steps 1–5 of "Wheel of Mystery Block Construction" to make a half block, using two dark A pieces, two light-medium B pieces, and one light-medium C piece. Sew another light-medium C piece to the A piece as shown. Clip 1" from the wide end of the C piece. Press the seam in the same manner as the other C seams. Join one dark A piece, one light-medium B piece, and one light-medium D piece as shown. Press the seams open. Sew the two units together. Clip 1" from the wide end of the C seam and press as you did for the previous C seams. Make 12.

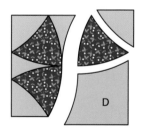

Block C.
Make 12.

3. Refer to step 2 to make block D using three medium A pieces, three white B pieces, two white C pieces, and one white D piece. Make eight.

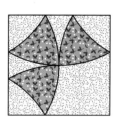

Block D.
Make 8.

4. To make block E, sew white and light-medium 5¼" triangles to the long sides of an H piece as shown. Press the seams open. Make 16.

Block E.
Make 16.

5. To make block F, sew a white K piece to the long edge of a J piece; then sew a light-medium 1¾" triangle to the short edge of the J piece as shown. Repeat to sew a J reversed piece, white K reversed piece, and light-medium 1¾" triangle together. Sew the two units together. Make four.

Block F.
Make 4.

6. Repeat step 5 with the remaining J and J reversed pieces, the light-medium K and K reversed pieces, and the white 1¾" triangles to make block G. Make four.

Block G.
Make 4.

7. If necessary, square up the blocks to 7½" x 7½", being careful not to cut off any of the points.

Assembling the Quilt Top

1. Arrange the blocks on the design wall as shown. Label the upper-left corner of each block with its row and position using a numbered self-adhesive dot. A digital picture of the block arrangement is also helpful.

2. Sew the blocks in each row together. Press the seams open. Sew the rows together, sewing each row from the opposite direction as the previous row to prevent distortion. Press the seams open.

Finishing

Refer to "Finishing Techniques" (page 22) as needed for assistance with any of the following steps.

1. Piece and cut the backing fabric so it measures 6" longer and 6" wider than the quilt top.

2. Layer the quilt top with batting and backing; baste.

3. Quilt as desired. For this quilt, the striped pieces were stitched ¼" from the edges. The A pieces were quilted with a furled ribbon design, while the background was quilted with a stipple stitch and an occasional free-motion four-petal flower.

   Note: If you pressed your seams open, *do not* stitch in the ditch. You'll only be stitching over thread since there is no seam allowance under the seam.

4. Block the quilt and let it dry. Trim away the excess batting and backing.

5. Bind the quilt edges with the binding-fabric strips.

6. Make a hanging sleeve, if desired, and stitch it to the backing.

7. Add a label and sign your quilt.

Patterns

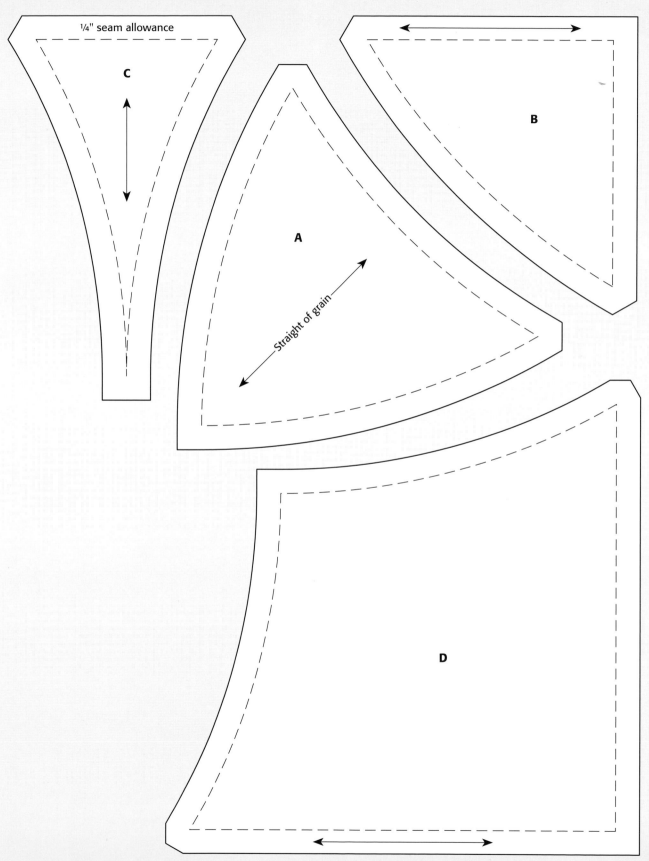

¼" seam allowance

C

A

Straight of grain

B

D

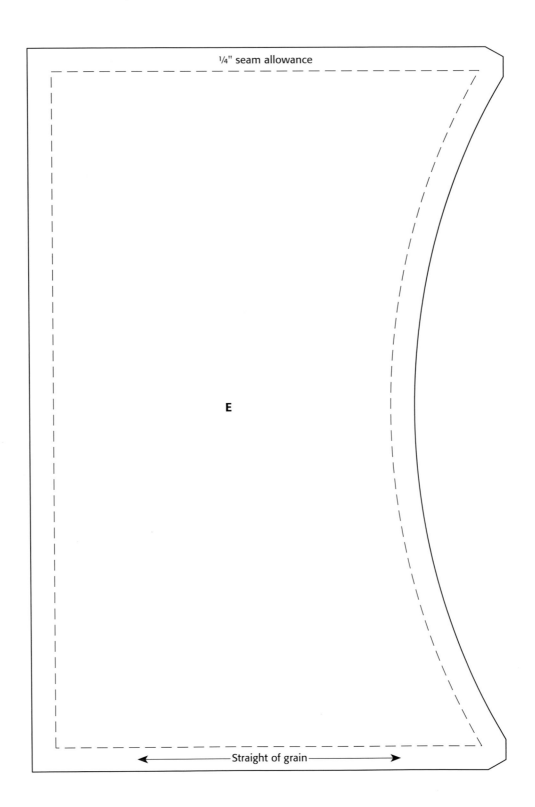

¼" seam allowance

E

Straight of grain

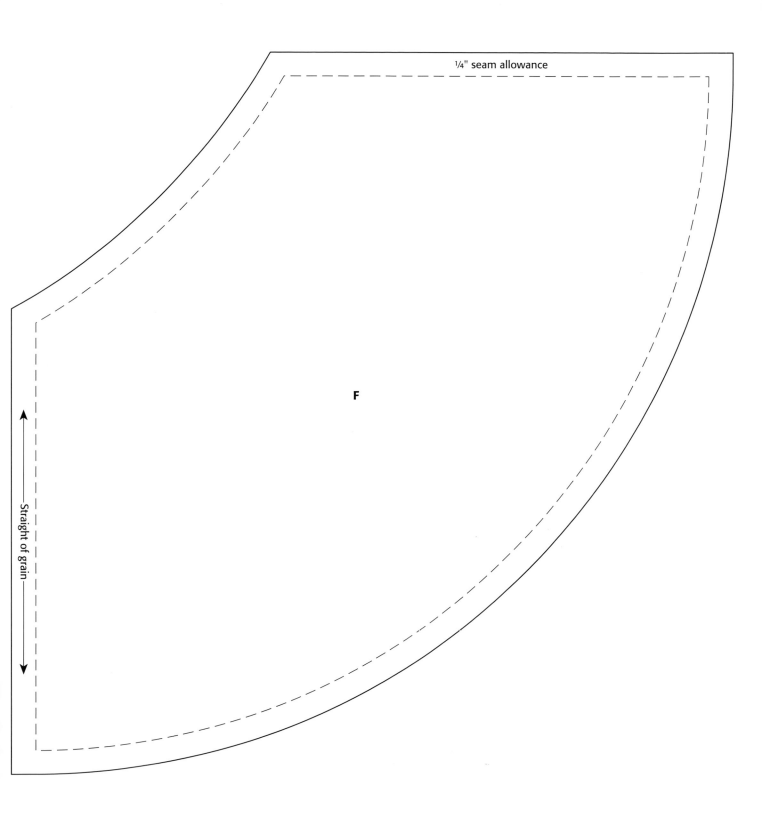

¼" seam allowance

F

Straight of grain

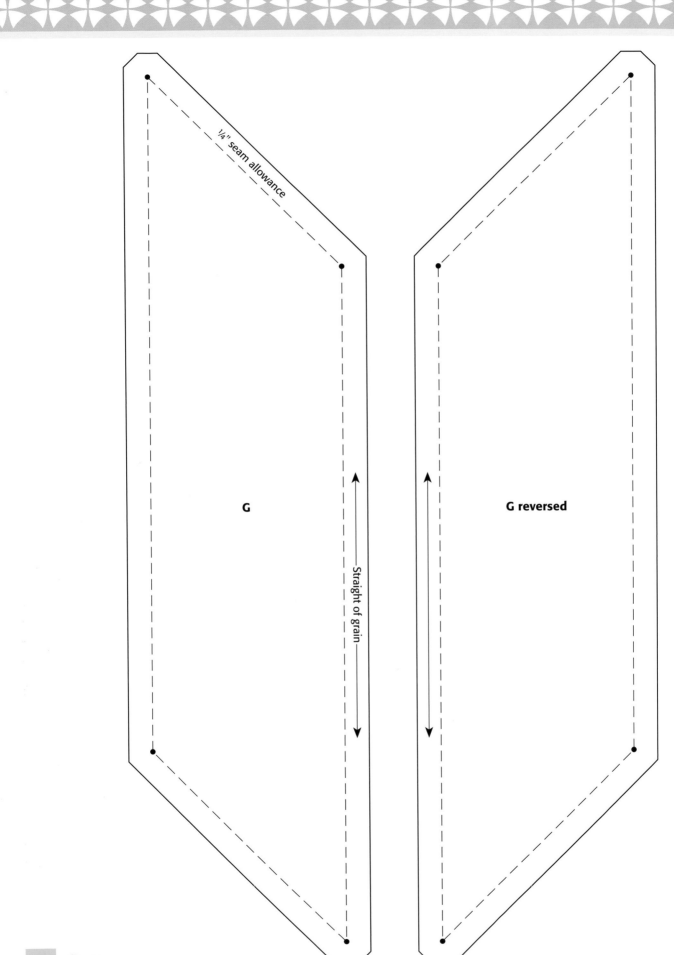

¼" seam allowance

G

Straight of grain

G reversed

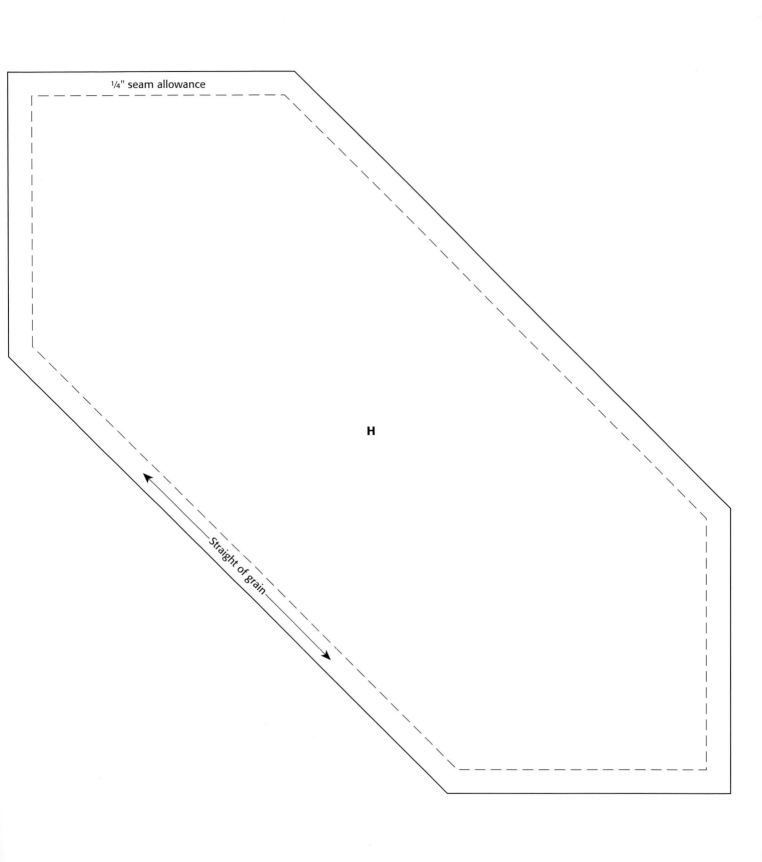

¼" seam allowance

H

Straight of grain

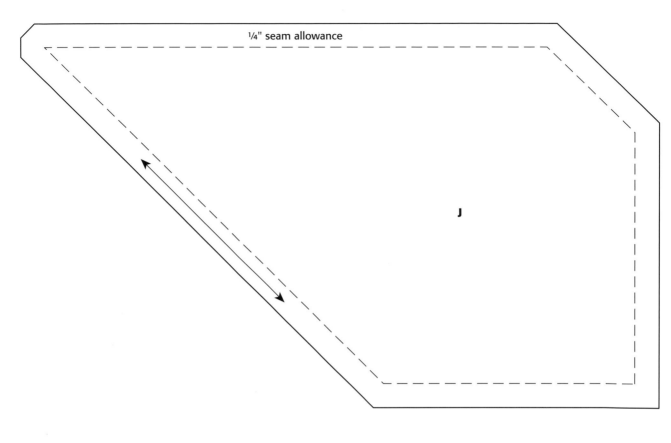

¼" seam allowance

J

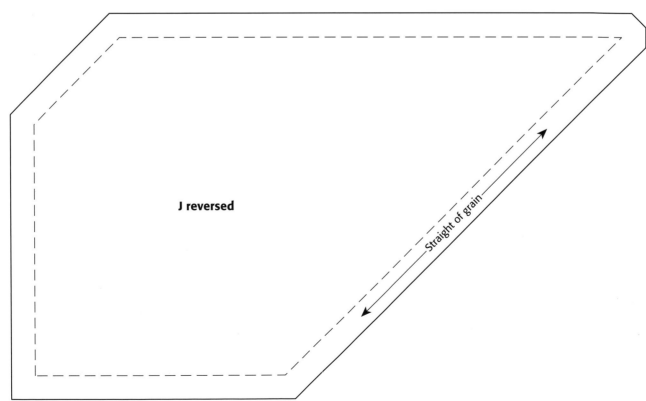

J reversed

Straight of grain

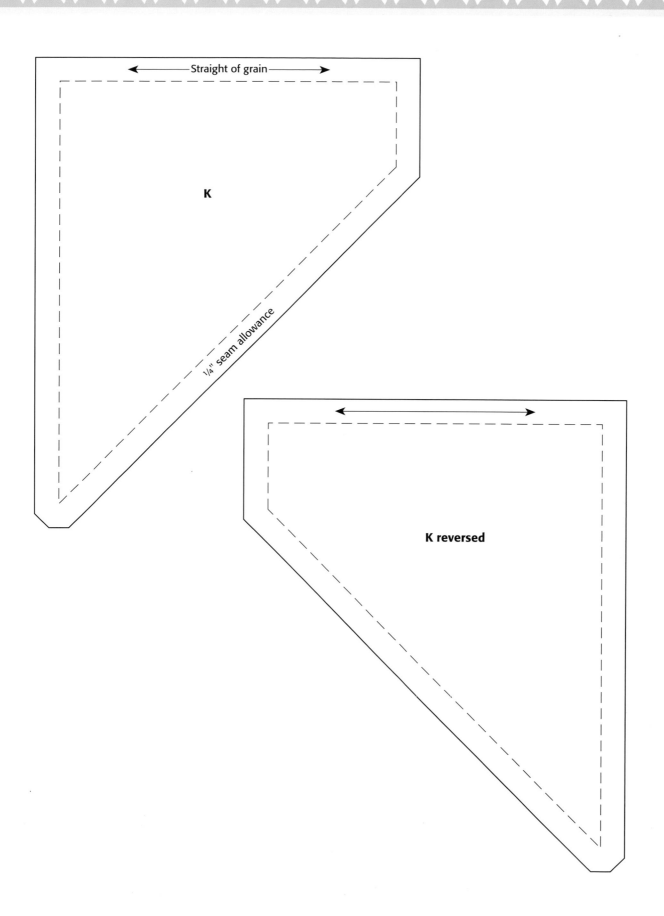

Straight of grain

K

¼" seam allowance

K reversed

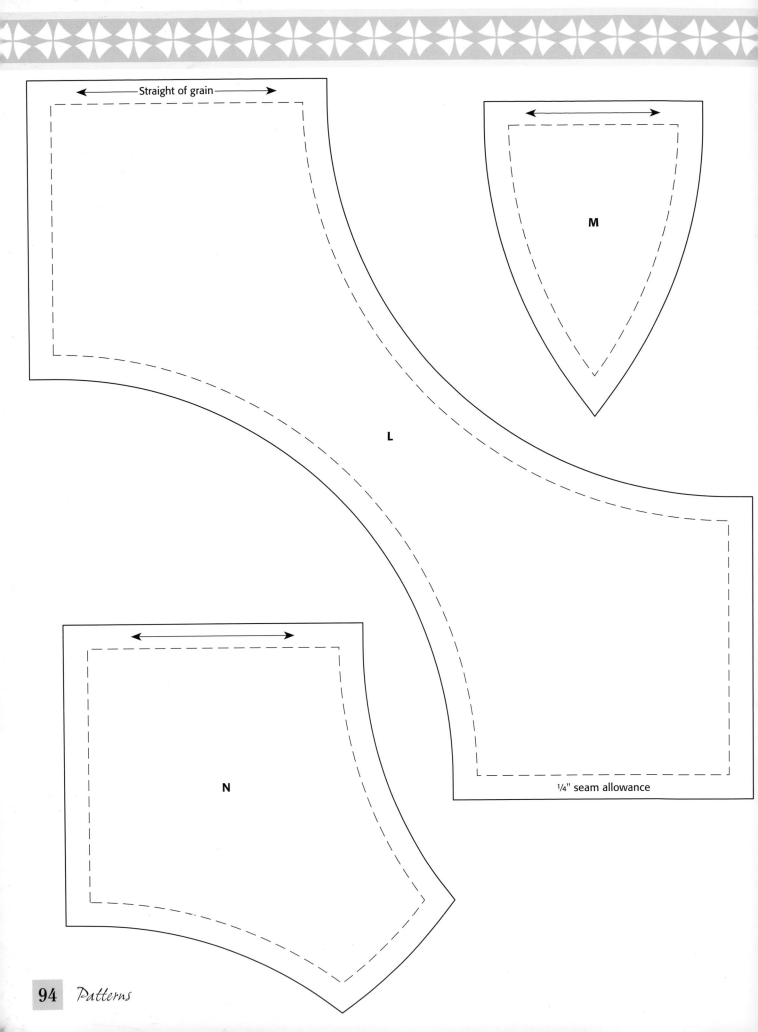

Straight of grain

M

L

N

¼" seam allowance

Resources

Scissors and cutting tools
Havel's Sewing Inc.
3726 Lonsdale St.
Cincinnati, OH 45227
Phone: (800) 638-4770
www.havelssewing.com

Fabrics and notions
International Fabric Collection
PO Box 72
Fairview, PA 16415
Phone: (800) 462-3891
www.intfab.com

Big Horn Quilts
529 Greybull Avenue
Greybull, WY 82426
Phone: (877) 586-9150
www.bighornquilts.com

Ami Simms
Mallery Press, Inc.
4206 Sheraton Drive
Flint, MI 48532
Phone: (800) 278-4824
www.AmiSimms.com

Quilt classes online
Quilt University
www.quiltuniversity.com

Quilt-design software
The Electric Quilt Company
419 Gould Street, Suite 2
Bowling Green, OH 43402
Phone: (800) 356-4219
www.electricquilt.com

Suggested Reading List

Barnes, Christine. *Color: The Quilter's Guide.* Woodinville, WA: That Patchwork Place, 1997.

Cleland, Lee. *Quilting Makes the Quilt.* Woodinville, WA: That Patchwork Place, 1995.

Dietrich, Mimi. *Happy Endings: Finishing the Edges of Your Quilt, Revised Edition.* Woodinville, WA: Martingale & Company, 2003.

Gaudynski, Diane. *Guide to Machine Quilting.* Paducah, KY: American Quilter's Society, 2002.

Nickels, Sue. *Machine Quilting: A Primer of Techniques.* Paducah, KY: American Quilter's Society, 2003.

Noble, Maurine. *Machine Quilting Made Easy!* Woodinville, WA: That Patchwork Place, 1994.

About the Author

Helen Marshall lives in New Zealand with her husband, Rodney. She has sewn all her life, starting with doll clothes when she was young and progressing to clothing for her family. When her now-adult children, Catherine and Neil, were in school, she attended embroidery and patchwork classes for several years.

As well as teaching both in and out of New Zealand and online for www.quiltuniversity.com, Helen curates exhibits of New Zealand quilts that travel to the United States. Helen's embroidery has been featured in *Inspirations* magazine, and will appear in the magazine's forthcoming book. Her large garden and the unique countryside of New Zealand are often an inspiration for her embroidery and quiltmaking. You can view Helen's web page at www.helenmarshalldesigns.com.